Explorations in World History

Niv Horesh

Explorations in World History

The Knowing of Globalization

Niv Horesh
The Louis Frieberg Center for East Asian Studies
Jerusalem, Israel

ISBN 978-981-99-4426-2   ISBN 978-981-99-4427-9 (eBook)
https://doi.org/10.1007/978-981-99-4427-9

© The Editor(s) (if applicable) and The Author(s), under exclusive license to Springer Nature Singapore Pte Ltd. 2023

This work is subject to copyright. All rights are solely and exclusively licensed by the Publisher, whether the whole or part of the material is concerned, specifically the rights of translation, reprinting, reuse of illustrations, recitation, broadcasting, reproduction on microfilms or in any other physical way, and transmission or information storage and retrieval, electronic adaptation, computer software, or by similar or dissimilar methodology now known or hereafter developed.

The use of general descriptive names, registered names, trademarks, service marks, etc. in this publication does not imply, even in the absence of a specific statement, that such names are exempt from the relevant protective laws and regulations and therefore free for general use.

The publisher, the authors, and the editors are safe to assume that the advice and information in this book are believed to be true and accurate at the date of publication. Neither the publisher nor the authors or the editors give a warranty, expressed or implied, with respect to the material contained herein or for any errors or omissions that may have been made. The publisher remains neutral with regard to jurisdictional claims in published maps and institutional affiliations.

Cover illustration: © Melisa Hasan

This Palgrave Macmillan imprint is published by the registered company Springer Nature Singapore Pte Ltd.
The registered company address is: 152 Beach Road, #21-01/04 Gateway East, Singapore 189721, Singapore

Contents

1	Introduction	1
2	Between World and Global History	7
3	The Empire Strikes Again: Will Nation States Wither Away?	15
4	Tracing the Cutting Edge of a Field Within World History	23
	Systems of Power	25
	Cultures of Power	31
	Disparities of Power	35
5	Establishing the Storylines	41
	Part I—Bronze to Iron Age	43
	Part II—The Classical Age	46
	Part III—The Ecumenical Turn	48
	Part IV—The Mongol Moment	50
	Part V—Another World	52
	Part VI—The Great Confluence	53
	Part VII—The Global Turn	55
	Part VIII—The 20th Century	59
	Overall Appraisal	61
	The Jewish Dimension	63

| 6 | Academics, Politicians, the Media and the Making of Modern China's Worldview | 65 |
| 7 | Conclusions | 77 |

CHAPTER 1

Introduction

Abstract World history is the most dynamic branch of academic historiography, and is, therefore, worth exploring. It is a branch of history that is dedicated to the study of history in more than one country at once, and often on a global scale. But it was really only the resurgence of China in the late 20th Century that reframed the profession as less Eurocentric. This was also the time when world history became more ecumenical with new textbooks and journals published in that area, encouraged by the late Jerry H. Bentley, the doyen of the field. Practitioners have since been organized for the most part within the World History Association. As opposed to global historians, world historians tend to de-emphasize individual nations, but they vary in their approach to time scales: some look for change over millennia, others focus on single years. Similarly, some world historians look at just one commodity of trade while others at many at once.

Keywords World history · Global history · Jerry H. Bentley

World history is the most dynamic branch of academic historiography, and is, therefore, worth exploring. It is a branch of history that is dedicated to the study of history in more than one country at once, and often on a global scale. Its forerunners included luminaries such as Herodotus (5th

Century BCE), Rashid a-Din (1247–1318), Ibn Khaldun (1332–1409), Montesquieu (1689–1755) and more recently, HG Wells (1866–1946). But it was really only the resurgence of China in the late 20th Century that reframed the profession as less Eurocentric. This was also the time when world history became more ecumenical with new textbooks and journals published in that area, encouraged by the late Jerry H. Bentley, the doyen of the field. Practitioners have since been organized for the most part within the World History Association.

Today, world history emphasizes in particular the identification of common patterns across different civilizations, as well as residual differences in a globalizing world. Increasingly, world history textbooks, which often go against the grain of ultranationalism, also replace those stressing the uniqueness of Western civilizations in schools and colleges. They invariably attempt to transcend the nation state as a Rankean unit of analysis and combat Eurocentric assumptions. World historians study networks and connections across linguistic boundaries, focusing on social phenomena such as migration and industrialization.

Hence, a world history study usually involves cultures that actually had contact and influence on one another, or cultures that went through various stages of development with little or no outside influence. World history tends to be more general, diachronic and comparativist than national histories. World historians seek connections between different civilizations on a macro level. When connections do not exist, they employ comparisons between the same civilizations.

World historians tend to de-emphasize individual nations, but they vary in their approach to time scales: some look for change over millennia, others focus on single years. Similarly, some world historians look at just one commodity of trade while others at many at once.

* * *

This book is in the first instance about the dynamics in the relatively new field of world history, which has grown infinitely in the last few years. But unlike other books, it focuses on comparative historical detail rather than on theory, resources or classroom gossip. There are now many more titles bearing the name x, y or z in world history, however, these are rarely contextualized under one roof. I will address the most important theoretical and case-study additions to the field, and so as to adduce best practice and common patterns in history. A particular emphasis will be placed on empires, and on China and the US as historical rivals. This book's approach is different also because it is framed around reviews that delve deep into the interior of some of the most important books in the field.

These books under review are all new or relatively new books so the narrative will remain cutting edge. The books will be organized in the following manner whereby I start with this Introduction to explain the contours of the field, then followed by a review of 6 important books that demonstrate my arguments. Again, the idea is that an in-depth review through meticulous critical readings of arguments and counter-arguments will elicit common patterns in world history both as the past and as a field of study. Throughout, I will aim to convey to wider readerships key common features in world history debates and tell them things they did not know about far-flung societies.

The books discussed are:

> Diego Olstein (2015), *Thinking History Globally* (Palgrave).
> Krishnan Kumar (2021), *Empire: A Historical and Political Sociology* (Polity Press).
> *The Oxford World History of Empire* (2021, 2 Vols.), Edited by Peter Fibiger Bang, C. A. Bayly and Walter Scheidel.
> Xin Fan (2021), *World History and National Identity in China: The Twentieth Century* (Cambridge University Press).
> Christopher A. Ford (2015), *China Looks at the West: Identity, Global Ambitions, and the Future of Sino-American Relations* (University of Kentucky Press).

The order of the reviews is not coincidental. It provides a sequence from theory-geared publications to more detail-geared ones. I end with a book taking us from the realm of world history to current affairs by way of demonstrating the significance of world history to the formation of one's national identity.

As will become evident, the difference between world history and global history or the history of globalization can be quite fluid. Empire studies by contrast are much more focused on a polity which John Darwin dubbed "the default mode of …most of history".[1] There is here emphasis

---

[1] John Darwin (2007), *After Tamerlane: The Global History of Empire* (Penguin), p. 23.

on empire studies as a sub-branch of world history because of that. Yet even when it comes to empire—pinning down which polity was or wasn't imperial is hard. There is also a vague demarcation line between modern and pre-modern empires that needs defining, as I attempt to do tentatively in the following pages.

Globalization as a temporal marker is what separates global history from world history "politically". Both can take up themes like climate change but the former is primed to explore the theme only in the last 500 years. The rationale is that globalization has radically changed the way we look at the past. This approach has much merit but it leaves out completely pre-modern empire formation which, I believe, has lessons for modern reader too. This is in a nutshell why the book is not titled "exploration in global history".

Having said that, I do recognize the significance of globalization: modern empires were in that sense a different "animal" that calls for innovative comparative and connective accounts. The books under review here will, therefore, examine the structures, processes and theories of global change with particular emphasis on economic detail. Phenomena like colonialism, imperialism, religion, migration, slavery and commerce will be mentioned. By employing a global prism, these yield insights not possible when one is limited to the national boilerplate.

Relying on the books reviewed, I zoom into the phenomenon of empire in world history from time immemorial, and by discussing many case studies at different eras, produce a non-Eurocentric (secondary) account of its evolution. That is to say, empire studies cannot be advanced by using just one or two case studies. In that sense, reading The *Oxford World History of Empire* and taking notes was an edifying process, and I feel privileged to be publishing a review thereof.

It is the first world history of empire, stretching back to the third millennium BC. Volume One is dedicated to synthesis and comparison. Following a comprehensive theoretical survey and bold world history synthesis, fifteen chapters analyze and explore the multifaceted experience of empire across cultures and through the ages. They do so with flying colors as will be explained in the following pages.

Volume Two pursues the protean history of political domination. Case studies here deal with the full range of the historical experience of empire, from the realms of the Achaemenids and Asoka to the empires of Mali and Songhay, and from ancient Rome and China to the Mughals, American settler colonialism and the Soviet Union. Forty-five chapters detailing the history of individual empires are—in the words of the publisher—tied together by a set of global synthesizing surveys that structure the world history of empire into eight chronological phases. This complex and rich Volume constitutes the core of my review sequence here.

The interplay between the process of globalization and the staying power of the nation state is slippery.

It is only through a multi-epoch assessment of empires that we can reach insights on the provenance and longevity of the Rankean historical construct of the nation state. Obviously, the latter is not as long lived as empire, yet from today's vantage point may prove more enduring. We need a historical base from which to peruse this imbalance. Are empires coming back to the fore of human destiny on the back of China's rise to determine human destiny? What do events like Brexit tells about the demise of large empire-like multi-ethnic bodies? And are the riots in Iran an offshoot of the Arab Spring or a state-centric event? The evidence is inconclusive but tapping the rich historical base can be productive in making informed guesses about the future. That the world every 4 years still mobilizes popularly, for example, along nation state lines during the FIFA World Cup is a testament to the staying power of the nation state.

Yes, the evidence is inconclusive but associated with the return or so-called return of empire is the notion that Eurocentrism may be bowing out from the historical front stage. For most of the empires the world has known were not European, while the nation state as a construct has a European pedigree. Already, the study of history is replete with myth-busting works designed to tell the story of globalization from the Global South. But, on the other hand, English firmly remains—even more so—the language of global academia. Precisely because of that, we need a book in English that will navigate the valleys and mountains of world history and global history relying on some of the most influential new works in these fields.

* * *

The book is organized as follows. It starts off with Olstein's theoretical foray demarcating the field of world history. It then continues with Kumar's theoretical treatise on empire. This is followed by the two volumes of The *Oxford World History of Empire*. Finally, I turn attention to the links between world history and national identity formation in China, drawing on Fan and Ford.

I end the book with China, because it was partly China's rise that begot the "global" turn in history in the 1990s. Fan argues that nationalism is pervasive in China today. Yet nationalism is not entrenched in China's intellectual tradition. Fan examines the ways in which historians working on the world beyond China from within China have attempted to construct narratives that challenge nationalist readings of the Chinese past and the influence that these historians have had on the formation of Chinese identity. He traces—in the words of the publisher—the ways in which generations of historians, from the late Qing through the Republican period, through the Mao period to the relative moment of "opening" in the 1980s, have attempted to break cross-cultural boundaries in writing an alternative to the national narrative.

Chinese leaders have long been fascinated by the US, but have often chosen to demonize it for perceived cultural and military imperialism. Especially under Communist rule, Chinese leaders have crafted and re-crafted portrayals of the US according to the needs of their own agenda and the regime's self-image—often seeing America as an antagonist and foil, but sometimes playing it up as a model. If Fan provides the scaffolding for the Chinese world vision, Ford provides the end result affecting politics. At a time China is rising fast often colliding with other countries' interest there is arguably no more urgent task than understanding the Chinese world vision better.

CHAPTER 2

Between World and Global History

Abstract For Olstein, good global history is about thinking outside the box, something that our own experiences in a globalized world have prepared us for. Yet, before the millennials, the study of history at high school was mostly circumscribed to one's country of birth; and the nation state persists as the key entity in our world, some might add. History writing, too, was until the 1990s deeply subsumed by the impact of the nation state, and research funding was accordingly earmarked. Globalization and state affiliation have since shaped our consciousness economically, socially and culturally. In a word, we partake of widening community circles, professional and otherwise.

Keywords Nation state · Olstein · Sprenger · Perón

Diego's Olstein's book (*Thinking History Globally*, Palgrave, 2015) concerns the "global" turn in the profession of history in the West, and therefore, it deals with many of the themes that were close to the heart of the late Jerry Bentley, the former doyen of the field. While bold and extensive in its coverage, the book is best understood as part of a group of recent studies all along these lines: these were penned or edited by Sebastian Conrad, Patrick Manning, Matthias Middell, Sven Beckert and

Dominic Sachsenmaier, and Roland Wenzlhuemer among others.[1] This is not to say that Olstein's *oeuvre* is unoriginal, on the contrary; only that its real value lies in the case studies and comparative data he compiles rather than the discussion of theory, which the others attend to too.

For Olstein, good global history is about thinking outside the box (p. 2), something that our own experiences in a globalized world have prepared us for. Yet, before the millennials, the study of history at high school was mostly circumscribed to one's country of birth (p. 4); and the nation state persists as the key entity in our world, some might add. History writing, too, was until the 1990s deeply subsumed by the impact of the nation state, and research funding was accordingly earmarked. Globalization and state affiliation have since shaped our consciousness economically, socially and culturally. In a word, we partake of widening community circles, professional and otherwise.

Before the 1990s, the only exceptions to the norm were the history of international relations, diplomacy and warfare which by definition are more geared to transnational research (p. 5). There were also precocious lateral thinkers whose research crossed boundaries in the 1930s like Wells, Spengler, Toynbee and Mumford but they lived in a Eurocentric age. By contrast, Olstein deals in the main with 21st-Century research that explicitly aims to transcend Eurocentrism. He proposes (p. 7) to evaluate that research and to set out a road map for best practice in the field, by invoking 12 branches of inquiry, and four approaches (comparing, connecting, conceptualizing and contextualizing). Here, I will only address those branches and approaches that in my view really matter in terms of category headings. Global history to me is both the overall field portmanteau and one of the 12 branches of inquiry thereunder.

Chapter 1 puts all of these branches and approaches to test within the context of the Juan Perón years in post-War Argentina. Olstein places (p. 10) particular emphasis on Perón's Non-Alignment credentials, something he shared with other leaders in the de-colonizing,

---

[1] Sebastian Conrad (2017), *What is Global History* (Princeton University Press); Patrick Manning (2003), *Navigating World History: Historians Create a Global Past* (Springer); Matthias Middel ed. (2019), *The Practice of Global History: European Perspectives* (Bloomsbury); Sven Beckert and Dominic Sachsenmaier eds. (2018), *Global History, Globally: Research and Practice around the World* (Bloomsbury); Roland Wenzlhuemer (2019), *Doing Global History. An introduction in 6 Concepts* (Bloomsbury).

developing world. Economic historians have studied his nationalization and import-substitution strategies but these—Olstein suggests—can be framed globally using his 12 branches.

Comparative history is a branch of global history that looks at two units at once. The most compelling case then would be to look at Perón vis-à-vis the Vargas regime in Brazil (p. 11). Other apposite cases are Nasser in Egypt, Sukarno in Indonesia, Nehru in India, Nkrumeh in Ghana, as well as Cardenas in Mexico, Betancourt in Venezuela, Arias in Panama and Ibarra in Ecuador (pp. 20–22). All these leaders, pursued nationalization of foreign assets, were elected democratically but became populists. Further afield, comparisons could be made with the UK (p. 15), which exerted immense economic influence on Latin America before World War II. It is no coincidence soccer, tennis and polo are still popular in Argentina, this is part of the British legacy there.

Transnational history is another branch of global history, and from that perspective Perón's sponsorship of Nazi migrants to Argentina can be pursued (p. 17). Still another branch, oceanic history, might call attention to the fact that most of Argentine exports after the War were freighted on foreign ships, predominantly British (p. 18). Hence, the Argentine landed elite was sympathetic to Britain, while lower classes complained about loss of control over distribution, prices and wages.

World history is yet another branch of global history but unlike the latter it encompasses inquiry into eras well before the current wave of globalization, which began arguably 500 years ago (p. 27). In other words, world history legitimates the study of history since the creation of planet earth 2.5 million years ago. But this is not to say the 12 branches are mutually exclusive. On the contrary, there is much epistemological overlap in the chapters to come.

Chapter 2 begins with the convolution of Roman history: Romulus, the city founder, established a monarchy, which became a republic in BCE 509, which then again—under Caesar—turned into a monarchy (p. 33). This is a warning against historical teleologies. Next, Olstein demonstrates the overlap that exists between the different branches mentioning key historians from Marc Bloch the comparativist to Sanjay Subrahmanyam, who is a relational theorist (p. 35). Relational historians, however, are the only ones among the group of 12 branches without a professional journal in which to publish. As for international history—this branch is the one most tied up with the nation state among the 12. Transnational history in turn is led by Harvard's Akira Iriye (p. 36).

Oceanic history was famously established by Braudel and furthered by Pierre Chaunu. Its journal is the *Journal of Maritime History*. Civilizational history had by contrast begun much earlier with the work of Vico, Motesquieu and Herder. Today, the leading journal in the field *is Comparative Civilization Review* (p. 39).

Historical sociology is a branch that dates back to Marx, Durkenheim and more recently Lipset. Here, scholars mainly deal with the rise of Capitalism worldwide, and the main publication vehicle is the *Journal of Historical Sociology* (p. 40).

Launched in 2005, the *Journal of Global History* is the marquee publication of the eponymous branch (p. 42). Here, the main luminary shaping the field in the formative years was the late Bruce Mazlish. Today, the field is led by scholars like Kevin O'Rourke and Anthony Hopkins. Its other publications are *Journal of New Global Studies* and *Itinerario*.

World history as sub branch of global history owes much to the work of William H. McNeill and Marshall G.S. Hodgson, and the establishment of the World History Association in 1982. More survey courses in world history are offered today at college level, and many of the textbooks here were written by affiliated scholars (p. 44). The marquee publication is the *Journal of World History*, established in 1990. Herein, classic-era scholars like Herodotus, Sima Qian, Rashid a-Din and Ibn-Khaldun are frequently mentioned. Established by David Christian in 1989, "big" history is the newest branch of global history (p. 46). Its forerunners were Alexander von Humboldt and Robert Chambers, but today it is dedicated to the history of the cosmos right down to the Big Bang.

Chapter 3 is about moving across disciplinary boundaries. From a civilizational point of you, one can easily see that ancient Sumer, for example, was politically fragmented, while Egypt was relatively united (p. 63). The question is how to account for that fact: Was it the navigability of the Nile that facilitated unification? The question is fascinating and relevant. However, Olstein is wrong to suggest here that Mesopotamia did not trade with Egypt at all—there was in fact some trade, as there was between Mesopotamia and the Indus Valley. Olstein then infers for readers: "comparing" as an approach in this case is about politics, while connecting is about trade links. McNeill, for example, transitioned through his career from comparing to connecting (p. 81).

It is conventionally thought that ancient empires lasted longer than modern ones. Olstein weighs into the debate by reminding us that Rome excelled in local elite acculturation, and this is why it lasted longer than the British or Spanish empires (p. 64).

Chapter 4 continues along the theme of comparing and connecting as research approaches. For comparative history more than one nation state is needed, and much the same applies to historical sociology (p. 88). Other branches zoom in on bigger units usually: civilizations, continents or the entire world. There are many journals that accept comparative-history articles and a few specialized ones (p. 90). A comparison of Latin and Chinese script, for example, might conclude that the former is simpler and therefore more democratic (p. 93). Yet by foregrounding the longevity of the Chinese empire, we might "provincialise" the significance of Latin script.

The best example for a stellar comparative history is Kenneth Pomeranz' *The Great Divergence*. Pomeranz invokes two key units of comparison, England and China, but *connects* them progressively to a wider socio-economic context of world proportions. So world history is ultimately his destination (p. 91). In his view, England overtook China economically due to its coal deposits which were situated along rivers and canals, and the colonial exploitation of American resources.

Chapter 5 deals with the varieties of connections in global history. Here, Olstein reminds us that the branches of international and transnational history are bounded up by nation states, thus militating researchers of that persuasion to focus on the last 200 years of history. In that sense, the scope for connection is limited (p. 100).

To demonstrate best practice in the field of transnational history, Olstein turns to Emily Rosenberg's work on pre-War US "dollar diplomacy" (p. 102). That is, American loans were given to a host of countries mainly in Latin America in exchange of the right to manage their customs, taxation and investment as well as for the adoption of the gold standard. This study of how the US sought to teach "natives" good economics has clear cultural connective dimension.

Another important study cited by Olstein is that of Marc Gallichio on African American attitudes to Japan following the Russo-Japanese war. By connecting two vastly different spheres, a minority community and a nation state on different continents, Gallichio shows how black internationalists hoped Japan would challenge white supremacy, thereby persuading the US government to abolish segregation. Black admiration for Japan skyrocketed after the World War I, when the Japanese representatives at the Versailles Peace Conference fought to include a resolution denouncing racism in the League of Nations charter (p. 103).

Oceanic history goes further beyond the nation state by "privileging bodies of water as units of analysis." This can sometimes apply also to lake or river settings, and is not restricted to the last 500 years (p. 106). The exemplary work Olstein cites here is KN Chaudhuri's *Trade and Civilization in the Indian Ocean* which includes a study of navigational technology and social attitudes to the sea amongst other topics (p. 110).

Chapter 6 is on conceptualization, an approach that was particularly important in sociologist Michael Mann's classic study on social power from time immemorial (p. 114). His analysis was based on the distinction between four main forms of power—political, economic, military and ideological—in different societies. In general, civilizational analysis of the sort Weber or Huntington performed is oriented toward sociology (p. 188). So too is world-system analyses that is preoccupied with demarcating exploitative core and periphery.

Chapter 7 is about Globalization. Here, Olstein returns (p. 125) to the subtle distinctions between global history and world history (p. 125). While these were spelt out in the *Journal of World History*, they remained silent in the *Journal of Global History*. The clearest indication of the distinction is perhaps the idea that global history as a branch means the history of globalization writ large. But here the burning question is precisely when globalization began ? "Extremists" suggest no earlier than the 19th Century, while moderates usually point to the discovery of the Americas as the watershed. The emergence of a "global" consciousness at any rate is a recent phenomenon. Flynn and Giraldez (p. 134) claim that by 1640 a price convergence had already occurred on the global silver market. So Globalization may be co-terminous with colonization (p. 139). After all, 125 of 188 UN members are former colonies.

Chapter 8 is about contextualizing on a bigger scale. Here, again Olstein addresses the difference between global and world histories. He notes (p. 140) that "world" is a polysemic word, while "globe" is not. We have Third World but no Third Globe, for example. So global history is singular, while world history encompasses pre-1500 history. In other words, the world of world history is "not predetermined", namely, it is not a deductive enterprise with a "top-down" scheme and a recognized beginning like the history of globalization.

In addressing Globalization, one has to consider not just Pomeranz' *Great Divergence* but also other divergences (p. 149) between continents that preceded 19th Century. The Greatest Divergence has to do with the lack of large mammals in pre-Columbian America as compared with Eurasia. The American Divergence is in turn about the higher standard of living that obtained in North America as compared with South America. Geographically, the Americas were less prone to the spread of germs because of their south-north axis while "horizontal" Eurasia had a richer biodiversity, as discussed by Jared Diamond.

Here, Olstein forgets to mention the Small Divergence, or the difference in the standard of living between Northwest and South Europe which widened as of the 17th Century. At any rate, when dealing with the Great Divergence, mention of big history is apt because (p. 152) this is the one branch that employs science in explaining pre-human and human lifeforms on planet earth. Yet big history shares some features with world history, not least in their college curriculum-driven inquiry, and engagement with the wider public.

The last chapter employs all of Olstein's 12 branches and four approaches (in inverted order) by way of revisiting World War I as a meta case study. The devil is in the detail here, though generalities are helpful more than theory. Olstein reminds (p. 157) us that in the lead-up to the War, industrializing France became dependent on Spanish rural goods. Spain thrived as a result during the War. Britain in turn became a debtor nation, and America a creditor nation after the War. Argentina stared industrializing too in order to offset shrinking agro-exports. It seems odd from today's vantage point perhaps but state intervention during the inter-War era became the norm till the emergence of neoliberalism in the 1970s (p. 166).

Olstein then proffers his own explanation for the Great Divergence. In his view (p. 171), it emanated from state competition in Europe versus singular political authority in China. That competition propelled maritime exploration and appetite for global dominance. But in terms of World War I, an inter-civilizational approach is more apt showing the impact of the war on non-combatants around the world. Oceanic history in turn would stress (p. 172) British concerns at Germany's naval build-up on the eve of the War.

The historical insights compiled by Olstein are probably more important in the long run than theory, as branches are a matter of fashion to some extent. Olstein's book itself is not just theory-driven but an exercise in world historiography. He rightly concludes by observing (p. 183): "In practice, what matters most is not adopting one branch or the other in an exclusive way but rather to embrace inclusiveness as a way to profit from all of them. Thinking globally is an inclusive project, and thinking history globally provides a solid base for understanding our global present".

CHAPTER 3

The Empire Strikes Again: Will Nation States Wither Away?

Abstract Kumar ably draws on almost all of the Western theoreticians on empire, from Hobson and Lenin to Luxemburg and Hilferding. If there is a subtext to Kumar's narrative, then it reveals itself gradually much to the enjoyment of the reader. And this subtext is to do with empires being more durable and longer-lasting than conventionally thought. Kumar also believes empires are not that dramatically distinct from the nation state.

Keywords Kumar · Empire · Jasper

Professor Krishnan Kumar has established himself as a thought leader in the field of empire studies. Notably, in 2017 he published the book *Visions of Empire* with Princeton University Press, which surveyed commonalities and differences between six empires: the Romans, the Ottoman empire, the Habsburg empire, the Russian empire, the British empire and the French empire. Those case studies reflected his inclinations and knowledge base at the time (p. x). Now, he has unfurled the canvass wider in space and time while aiming at conciseness all the same.

That is to say that the narrative under review (*Empire: A Historical and Political Sociology*, Polity Press, 2021) conveniently measuring 150 pp. seeks out the so-called pattern of empire by meticulously researching a greater set of case studies including China and India. Following a trenchant preface, the Volume is divided into 6 chapters: Chapter 1 presents the historical contours of empires, distinguishing between pre-modern and modern ones. Chapter 2 looks at the concept of *translatio imperii* or the ways and means by which present empires appropriate the mystique of past empires. Chapter 3 explains among other things the tension between metropole and periphery. Chapter 4, the most lucid of all, problematizes the distinction between empire and the nation state. Chapter 5 recounts the various factors behind the decline of empires. Finally, Chapter 6 broadly surveys the relevance of empire to today's world.

To anticipate the *finale*, Kumar ably draws on almost all of the Western theoreticians on empire, from Hobson and Lenin to Luxemburg and Hilferding. If there is a subtext to Kumar's narrative, then it reveals itself gradually much to the enjoyment of the reader. And this subtext is to do with empires being more durable and longer-lasting than conventionally thought. Kumar also believes empires are not that dramatically distinct from the nation state.

Following John Darwin, Kumar starts off by observing that empire is the commonest polity in recorded history (viii). Its mechanics preoccupied some of the brightest minds in times past from Herodotus, through Ibn Khaldun to Edward Gibbon. It also invited sharp criticism from the likes of Frantz Fanon and Edward Said. Kumar then observes that there is today popular nostalgia for empire. To be sure, as late as 1912 Indian leaders wanted the subcontinent to become part of a global empire (pp. 69–70). His more current proofs are books by Niall Ferguson and a TV series with Jeremy Paxman on the British empire. To wit, 59% of Britons say they are proud of the achievements of the British empire (p. 140). In Turkey, China and Russia too the imperial past is being rehabilitated. It is no longer cast as feudal or autocratic.

Equally, one might add, there is boisterous opposition to Tukey's neo-imperial ambitions both in the Arab world and within the country itself. In Southeast Asia, policymakers dread a return to a Chinese tributary agenda. In Scandinavia, there is real fear of Russia's turn to expansionism. And above all, the Black Lives Matter movement suggests there is no nostalgia for British empire in the periphery.

To his credit, Kumar recognizes that empires are not monolithic—they come in all shapes and sizes (pp. 1–2). As Richard Koebner observed, the word itself carried different meanings at different times—*imperium* in the Roman republican era simply meant absolute rule. It only later assumed the meaning of rule over a multiplicity of people. Outside the West, there was a host of words to designate empire with varying connotations (p. 5)—the Chinese *Tianxia* tributary order immediately comes to mind. Today, empire can designate any powerful organization from Google to Manchester City FC.

Kumar likes to deploy Jaspers' famous but somewhat problematic "Axial Age" trope to stress how religion and empire formation were inseparably linked in antiquity (pp. 9, 11). This is particularly questionable as regards the emergence of Rome, well before Christianity came on stream. And in that context, that the growth of Buddhism in China was a result of official Han imperial sponsorship is questionable (p. 10).

Whether universal transcendental thought was a pre-condition for the creation of empire in antiquity or not, Kumar provides a neat summary of other empires from Sumer, Egypt, Akkad, through to Assyria, Babylon and the Hittite empire (pp. 7–8). Kumar states that these empires by comparison lacked a universalist ideology; they were merely preoccupied with occupation and domination (p. 12). Yet, much like Chinese emperors, the Assyrian emperor was likened to a son of heaven (*mar banuti*), a universalist epithet.

Quick forward and, rightly, Kumar draws clear distinction between pre-modern empires and modern ones. As Adam Smith observed, the discovery of the Americas was a watershed in history. Notably, pre-modern empires were land based, modern empires had blue navies to straddle the ocean. And while the Phoenician empire in antiquity was also ocean going it was "loosely knit" (pp. 14–15). However, one might add, Carthage was better knit, operating as it did silver mines in its Iberian colonies.

Generally, a sense of commodities and a smidgen of economic history seem to be lacking at this point—when dealing with the Portuguese modern empire for example there is no mention of Indian black pepper and cloth (pp. 17, 20). Portugal matters not least because it was the first of the modern empires and the last to renounce it in 1974 (p. 22).

America is perhaps an empire in disguise whereas China was first called an "empire" (*diguo*) in Chinese only in the waning years of the Qing dynasty. It seems Kumar hints here that empires are nowadays so-called only in their terminal state (pp. 31–33). For empire has become a dirty word. That is perhaps a positive omen for the continuation of American dominance in the world.

Aside from confusing *pinyin* and Wade-Giles transliteration, Kumar's overview of Chinese imperial history is very crisp. The only mistake I could find had to do with Xiongnu nomads coveting Han-grown tea when in fact tea spread in China only later in the Tang era. It is also questionable whether the Tang empire was more territorially ambitious than the Han empire (p. 37) when the two were similar in size.

When it comes to the makeup of empire, while its rulers were mostly hereditary monarchs, republics could engender empires too, as the Roman precedent suggests. There were others later on: Venice and the Netherlands are two of the most salient. Athens may be too (p. 49). Even in the Holy Roman Empire, rulers had to receive elector consent.

Kumar rightly does not overdo the differences between land and sea empires. Both types of empire, while expanding, were generally aware the people they conquered often were legatees of a rich cultural heritage. Only Native Americans and Africans were derided as people "without history" (pp. 55, 68). One might also add Australian aborigines.

There was tension though between supremacist sentiments and anxiety for the future of empire. This is a duality that rhetorically dates back to Virgil and Tacitus in the Roman empire.

Kumar at any rate seems to suggest that land empires were somewhat more accommodating of local custom than sea empires (p. 61). Here, one might add that the Jesuits who worked on behalf of various European powers did generally accommodate local customs. A few other luminaries even admired "native" culture—Las Casas, Lord Curzon and Hubert Lyautey are notable examples (p. 66).

Kumar then maybe getting the figure wrong when stating 80% of current US population is white. In fact, non-Hispanic whites make up only 60% of the population (p. 62). These figures are essential if we were to understand the emergence of what I dubbed elsewhere "empires from within". That is to say, core-periphery relations in the nation state are nowadays shifting to remind us of an imperial structure, albeit with stationary borders.

The generalization that the freer white settlers were, the harsher they treated the local population (pp. 63–65) is also problematic. For the Boers who were less free than British settlers in South Africa were notorious in their attitude to Africans. And more generally minorities in imperial structures are usually subject to a pecking order depending on loyalty to the core.

* * *

This world belongs to nation states. However, there are some 8000 nations and only 193 members in the UN. Nations share ancestry, definite borders and a common language, and it is clear not all UN members fit the bill (p. 73). In particular, the UN includes city states and principalities but not the EU.

Barak Obama and Rishi Sunak aside, in most nation states the leader is of the same ethnicity as the core group. In empires by contrast the ruler usually reigns over a large population of ethnicity different to his. Due to this ethnic divide, empires were once thought to constitute an obstacle to modernization (p. 75). Yet it is often forgotten that in England a quasi-foreign dynasty presided over industrialization—the Hanovers. By extension there is no reason to believe empires are backward.

The case for empire is then reinforced by minimizing the difference between them and nation states. Kumar is at his best here. He eloquently shows how some nation states are really composite, not unitary, much like empires. If one were to look in fact at the history of most Western European states in their pre-imperial stage, one could find unadulterated fragmentation and counter-expansionism. The *locus classicus* is Britain which was formed through a multi-ethnic union with Wales, Scotland and Ireland (p. 77). This mode persists elsewhere, and in fact many UN members today are federal: Canada, Germany, India and the US to name but few. China and Russia are by definition multi-ethnic (p. 79).

So the unitary nation state is something of chimera one might add. That is because in the early 20th-Century imperialism and nationalism fused (p. 82). What is more, empires sometimes stirred up one form of nationalism so as to counter another. The best-known case is how Britain exacerbated tensions between Hindus and Muslims (p. 87).

* * *

The nature of power has changed too. There has been a debate in the pertinent scholarly literature as to whether pure economics drove 19th–20th-Century imperialism. Whatever the answer, my reading into Cold War history made me realize that the historical notion of empires is not synonymous with contemporary super-powerdom. This is mainly because of the implications of nuclear weaponry as a game changer.

Immerwahr in his magisterial *How to Hide an Empire* (Random House, 2019) has recently suggested that, on balance, other US technological breakthroughs during the post-war era made formal empire unattractive in view of the rising tide of national liberation movements worldwide. First, greater blue water mobility through, for example, the Panama Canal and aircraft carriers made holding on to large swathe of territory with ground forces less compelling. Faster planes have made the deployment of ground forces easier too. In the pre-war era, European colonies in the tropics had been otherwise indispensable in providing raw materials: for example, rubber for automobile tires. Other vital "colonial" commodities included West African palm oil as lubricant, Indian jute for packaging and off-shore Peruvian guano as fertilizer. All of those were partly replaced by synthetic materials in the 20th Century.

Kumar does not discuss Immerwahr's ideas, particularly the notion that technological advances and nationalism were driving the reconfiguration of empire. But by p. 90, his approach becomes clear in that he asserts that a world of competing nation states (federal or not) risks nuclear proliferation and conflict more than was the case in the imperial age (p. 90). This is something not all readers would agree with. In fact, there is evidence that warfare in the world under current governance arrangements is steadily subsiding. What's more, events like the Olympics or FIFA World Cup suggest nation states still draw on profound popular vein; they arouse identification arguably more than empires could.

Similarly, the decline of empire in the 20th Century is told rather optimistically, while discounting the power of nationalism, ecological and economic factors (p. 106). Kumar is right though that all empires, however long lasting, are bound to fail eventually like the "human body" (98). But in explaining the fall of the Qing dynasty for example, he misses short-circuits in the sinews of power, like so many bankruptcies of *guandu shangban* enterprises (p. 100). There is otherwise little on the bureaucracy, military organization or tax collection. What is more, in explaining Latin American emancipation, Kumar denies agency from Bolivar suggesting instead that Spain was weakened by Napoleon's invasion hence it relinquished colonial powers. (p. 108) In short, interimperial war rather than nationalism accounts for the looks of today's world (p. 113). This of course cannot explain the bitter anti-colonial struggle in Africa in the latter part of the 20th Century.

Certainly, empire bequeathed us many good things: a common language, a common calendar, railroads, and perhaps it might even be partly credited with the spread of monogamy. Yet empires can be very repressive too stretching right back to Assyria. This is why the nostalgia for empire should be taken with a grain of salt.

As mentioned, Kumar touches on the various streaks of imperial nostalgia though it is not clear how popularly embedded these are (pp. 121–13). In Austria, for example, it seems there is no burning desire to restore the Habsburg monarchy. Yet in Turkey there is deeper restorationist sentiment usually called neo-Ottomanism. What is more, former British dominions are edging closer and closer toward republicanism. Certainly, Brexit did not unleash much enthusiasm for restoring imperial connections (p. 57).

Whether multiculturalism is indeed "dead" following 9/11 is moot, and it is unclear—if so—whether empire is the answer (p. 139). The ottoman *millet* system may have been very ethnically tolerant and is a model for posterity (p. 142). But in treating empire we must not forget the greatest sins of all, slavery, as well as the extermination of Native Americans by force and through disease. Then there are issues like the Armenian genocide where responsibility falls evenly between empire and nation state. Stalin and his gulags fall into the same category too perhaps.

Kumar concludes by reiterating that nation states cannot simply be the be-all end-all of history because they spread anarchy and violence (p. 149). However, COVID-19 has shown that in times of crisis composite structures like the EU revert by default to their nation state constituents. The spread of one-man one-vote democracy also suggests horizontal association is on the rise. All of this throw into question the viability of empire at least in its previous iteration. Whatever may be the case, the book under review is lively; beautifully and tightly written with only few omissions. Kumar has penned a compelling defense of empire that is likely to become a classic in the field.

CHAPTER 4

Tracing the Cutting Edge of a Field Within World History

Abstract A younger generation of scholars has begun theoretically building on classics such as Doyle or Eisenstadt's, armed with much better case studies to analyze. And so by 2016 appeared what was then the most ambitious ecumenical project in the field, *The Encyclopedia of Empire*, edited by John Mackenzie. Notably, the *Encyclopedia* included many discursive essays on the pattern of key empires in addition to countless entries on better and lesser known empires. Mackenzie's feat is today caught up by an even more ambitious and extensively researched project, The *Oxford World History of Empire* consisting of a set of two volumes (edited by Peter Fibiger Bang, the late C. A. Bayly and Walter Scheidel, Oxford University Press, 2021). Because of the set's length, we will focus in this chapter on Volume One. All contributors to this Volume take a non-Eurocentric comparative approach covering every corner of the globe in the past 5000 years. This approach suggests *in toto* that empire is a more historically resilient polity than other forms including what may be a fleeting nation state modality.

Keywords *The Encyclopedia of Empire* · The *Oxford World History of Empire* · Peter Fibiger Bang, C. A. Bayly · Walter Scheidel

David Christian suggested that 19th-Century empiricism and nationalism made historians shun bigger-picture historical studies, militating instead for archival research on clearly defined local topics well into the next century. Yet, since the establishment of the *Journal of World History* in the 1990s more and more historians have taken advantage of the body of local research that has infinitely grown, as well as new scientific methodologies, so as to unfurl their canvass wider.[1]

Jerry Bentley, the founder of the journal, observed in the same vein that even 20th-Century historiography had been blighted by Eurocentrism and an obsession with nation state teleology, which then-emerging scholars like Bin Wong sought to correct. These younger historians' toolkit was in turn greater connectedness and attention to inter-civilizational encounters.[2]

In recent years, one of the most dynamic fields within this new more inclusive World History has proven to be the study of empires. This is of course not to say that path-breaking studies in this field did not occur earlier—Michael Doyle and Shmuel Eisenstadt are perhaps two of the best known.[3] However, Doyle was criticized for Eurocentrism (he hardly included China in his study) and Eisenstadt relied on the inaccurate scholarship available at the time.[4]

A younger generation of scholars has begun theoretically building on classics such as Doyle or Eisenstadt, armed with much better case studies to analyze. And so by 2016 appeared what was then the most ambitious ecumenical project in the field, *The Encyclopedia of Empire*, edited by John Mackenzie. Notably, the *Encyclopedia* included many discursive essays on the pattern of key empires in addition to countless entries on better and lesser known empires.[5]

---

[1] David Christian (2010), "The Return of Universal History", *History and Theory* 49, pp. 6–27.

[2] Jerry H. Bentley (2011), "The Task of World History" in idem. ed. *The Oxford Handbook of World History* (Oxford University Press), available at: https://www.oxfordhandbooks.com/view/10.1093/oxfordhb/9780199235810.001.0001/oxfordhb-9780199235810-e-1.

[3] Michael W. Doyle (rep. 2018) *Empires* (Cornell University Press); Shmuel N. Eisenstadt (1963) *The Political System of Empires* (Free Press).

[4] Hilde de Weerdt (2016), "Shmuel N. Eisenstadt and the Comparative Political History of Pre-Eighteenth-Century Empires", *The Asian Review of World Histories* 4.1, pp. 133–63.

[5] John M. Mackenzie ed. (2016), *Encyclopedia of Empire*, 4 Vols. (Wiley).

Mackenzie's feat is today caught up by an even more ambitious and extensively researched project, The *Oxford World History of Empire* consisting of a set of two volumes (Edited by Peter Fibiger Bang, the late C. A. Bayly and Walter Scheidel, Oxford University Press, 2021). Because of the set's length, we will focus in this Chapter on Volume One. All contributors to this Volume take a non-Eurocentric comparative approach covering every corner of the globe in the past 5000 years. This approach suggests *in toto* that empire is a more historically resilient polity than other forms including what may be a fleeting nation state modality.

Volume One (*The Imperial Experience*) covers theory and comparisons, broadly speaking, while Volume Two focuses on specific imperial histories, and is meant to throw back empirical sidelight on preceding discussions. The first, comparative Volume includes 15 chapters on scale, world systems and geopolitics, military organization, political economy and elite formation, monumental display, law, mapping and registering, religion, literature, the politics of difference, resistance, energy transfers, ecology, memories and the decline of empires. These are grouped into 3 subsections: systems of power, cultures of power and disparities of power.

Volume Two (*The History of Empires*) is by contrast an exhaustive assembly of case studies. It includes 45 chapters on empires from the very beginnings of state formation in the Bronze Age up to the present. The chapters here are—in the words of the publisher—tied together by a set of synthesizing surveys that structure the world history of empire into eight chronological phases. There is useful cross-referencing across the set but of the two volumes. One is the more important at least insofar as the epistemological foundation of the field is concerned.

SYSTEMS OF POWER

What is an empire? As trenchantly explained by Mackenzie it is basically an expansionist polity preoccupied with maintaining power for its "core" area primarily through military means. Expansionism usually plays out through military occupation but sometimes the coaxing of allies, contingent land purchases or marriage of nobles can equally bring about territorial growth.[6] "Core" usually suggests urban hubs where imperialists display their grandeur to mark them out as justifiably superior. And military outlay is paid for mainly through the exaction of agricultural tribute from occupied areas. Because it seeks to assert dominion over other ethnicities in the "periphery", empire is composite and multicultural almost by definition. All the rest is subject to administrative and ideological variation. To be sure, empires can even be so without having an emperor—a few republics turned into empires in history.[7]

Almost by definition, therefore, empires are hierarchical while exhibiting varying degree of local elite participation in the periphery. That is to say, empires can co-opt or assimilate peripheries, but also alienate them or fear being assimilated by them. By the same token, the "core" can be federal rather than unitary—the UK, or the Ayyubid dynasty are all cases in point.[8]

As for urban hubs, ancient Chinese and Pharaonic capital cities constituted less of an imperial core. In both cases the empire was more culturally uniform; the religious and political realm fused together, and the reign of emperors was absolute. China, though, possessed less of a hereditary nobility in the long run. While the Chinese "core" was mostly (but not always) made up of civil bureaucrats, the "core" in Europe was often aristocracies surmounting narrow imperial or ethnic divisions.[9] Hence, for example, the ambivalence shown in contemporary Britain about the Hanovers, and in Austria about the Austro-Hungarian multi-ethnic heritage.

Empires at any rate require strong ideological justifications often based on creation myths and linkages with antiquity to claim universal power. The best-known concept in this regard is *Translatio imperii* which suggested Frankish power was hitched right down to Alexander the Great. More concrete justification derived from the provision of public goods

---

[6] Chase-Dunn and Khutkyy in the volume under review also suggest (p. 146) that gift giving and marriage alliances whereby a headman married the daughter of another headman were rife in early empires.

[7] John Mackenzie (2016), "Introduction", in the *Encyclopedia of Empire* (Wiley), available at: https://onlinelibrary.wiley.com/page/book/10.1002/9781118455074/homepage/custom_copy.htm.

[8] Ibid.

[9] Stephen Howe (2002), *Empire: A Very Short Introduction* (Oxford University Press), p. 50.

like common language, highways, coinage, post and a legal system.[10] All of the above means that nation states as a 19th-Century construct are the foil against which empires are measured. Nation states seek homogeneity of the people within their midst and fixed borders for the most part. In that sense, nation states are seemingly more self-effacing and stationary than empires.[11]

* * *

The Volume under review begins with a 88-page prolegomena by Peter Fibiger Bang, one of the 3 editors. Eruditely expanding on many of the foregoing points, he clearly sets the stage for the syntheses to come, including with his own thorough discussion of the modern theories of imperialism—Marxist and non-Marxist alike. To cut to the chase, like in his earlier work Bang suggests empire whether in Eurasia or elsewhere is all about tribute (p. 64).[12] That is to say that next to military capacity ensuring their survival, empires were busy exacting agricultural tribute from the population they ruled, which was made possible largely by co-opting local elites. Like Mackenzie, Bang suggests that exacting tribute invites rebellion hence the need for constant military mobility.

Bang insightfully observes in his synthesis of theories (p. 48):

> Economically, empire appeared as a form of monopoly power, which exacts resources and draws rents from protection. Politically, empire was revealed to rely on compulsory cooperation, harnessing select and privileged elites from subject societies, who performed the tasks of local government for the metropolis in return for a share in the 'spoils of conquest and domination.'

---

[10] Hilde de Weerdt (2016), "The Diverging Legacies of Classical Empires in China and Europe", *European Review* 24.2, pp. 306–324 ff. 306–8; on highways see Thomas T. Allsen (2011), "Pre-modern Empires" in Jerry H. Bentley ed., *The Oxford Handbook of World History* (Oxford University Press), pp. 361–378, f. 367.

[11] See Haldon in the volume under review p. 182. Greece, Sumer and the Indus Valley may be described as proto nation states where elites shared ethnicity and common language; on the tension between empire and nation state see also Krishnan Kumar (2010), "Nation-states as Empires, Empires as Nation-states: Two Principles, One Practice?", *Theory and Society* 39, pp. 119–143.

[12] Peter Fibiger Bang and C. A. Bayly (2011) eds., *Tributary Empires in Global History* (Palgrave).

When it comes to the lifespan of empires Bang is maximalist. Decolonialization, Bang reminds us, and the ever-mounting number of newly formed nation states arising from the downfall of the USSR may indicate empires are a thing of the past. Yet the USSR itself was an empire even if Stalin was not an emperor by name. US imperial ambitions were by comparison less territorial but carried universalist claims nevertheless (p. 76).

One way of qualifying empire is to look at territory size, but there is disagreement in the field about the cut-off below which polities are merely kingdoms or city states. Against this background Walter Scheidel offers the second chapter with illuminating original data analysis.

Scheidel cautions us, however, that imperial borders were notoriously hard to pin down in the pre-modern age (pp. 89, 98). The militaries assembled to occupy land were otherwise dissimilar: the Mauryan empire relied on chariots and elephants while Qin China and Rome relied largely on infantry. The Roman military enjoyed more autonomy than in China.

Scheidel tells us (p. 102) that—amazingly—the Romans, Kushans and the Han empires covered together 2/3 of the world population at the time, a feat unsurpassed since. Generally, the post-Roman era in Europe saw much more political fragmentation than in East Asia whereas South Asia was in between (p. 106). One might add that Qin, China's first empire, was the outcome of states competing inward, while the Roman empire developed outward from a republic rife with slavery.[13] Scheidel's other main finding is that empires were generally bigger and more populous in China and South Asia than in Europe. This is an aspect of the so-called Great Divergence between polities that we cannot afford to ignore.

The third contribution in this section by Christopher Chase-Dunn and Dmytro Khutkyy is on the geopolitics of imperial systems. Like many others they observe (p. 116) that commodification changed the logic of geopolitics and fiscal planning not just in the modern era. Moreover, while most empires were agrarian in nature, there were in antiquity and the medieval era lesser powers based on trade (p. 129).

An early example is Dilmun, a city state situated in present-day Bahrain that tapped traffic between the Indus Valley and the Fertile Crescent. One might add the Phoenicians were traders too, although their colonies were

---

[13] Hilde de Weerdt (2016), *op. cit.*, p. 308.

less connected to a metropole as compared with modern colonies.[14] In medieval times, the Hanseatic League, the Italian city states and Novograd also come to mind. All of this is reminiscent of powerful city states in the contemporary world that is based on trade and finance, Singapore being an obvious example, and so is Luxembourg.

Chase-Dunn and Khutkyy suggest that territory size was all-important in the pre-modern age, while today's empires have a more limited core (p. 135). The stationary flair of empires in the contemporary world owes much to the triumph of the Westphalian model outside Europe, and to the sanctification of national sovereignty.

Chapter 4 by Ian Morris is on military organization. He usefully starts off by postulating that managing violence is "the job number one" for empires (p. 155). Polities lacking an army cannot count as empires, the EU included presumably. So too those spanning less than 1 million sq km (p. 156).

Morris then insightfully observes (p. 157) that military outlay is invariably the biggest item in imperial budgets, only that modern empires are also committed to large social welfare outlay so as to, in part, normalize citizenry. One might also add that revenue sources have changed: poll tax and tribute in the pre-modern age vs. corporate and income tax today. Pre-modern rulers captured only 2 to 3 percent of GDP in taxes, while the figure is closer to 50 percent in modern states (p. 163). Nevertheless, one might conclude modern armies are usually professional and much smaller than pre-modern armies as a ratio of tax receipts.

One might add that it is beyond doubt that the military outlay of keeping colonies at bay was immense, particularly in non-white colonies. And not once European colonialists lost with many casualties to count—for example, the Dutch in Taiwan, the Russian in Crimea, the Italians in Ethiopia, and the British in Zululand and Afghanistan. But, generally speaking—apart from the American War of Independence—colonial military outlay paled compared with the cost of warfare *within* Europe itself in the early modern era.[15]

---

[14] Carthage may have been an outlier in the pre-modern world in that it exploited colonial mines in Spain. Conventionally, colonies then were thought to have weaker links with the metropole.

[15] Stephen Howe (2002), *op. cit.*, p. 95; Niall Ferguson's (2004), *Empire: The Rise and Demise of the British World Order* (Basic Books), p. 247, suggests military outlay made

Morris sensibly goes on to identify the dilemma of cutting military outlay at the risk of engendering mutinies. In turn, increasing military outlay might militate the empire toward excessive plunder and resultant rebellion (p. 164), as well as rampant debasement. The classic example for such plunder-hungry empire is Assyria but Morris adds Zhou China and Rome too (p. 162). The Chinese in particular, one might add, had strategies in place to avert rebellion including stationing royal relatives away from the capital city, prohibitions on the service of royalty in the bureaucracy, and a ban on officials serving in their native places.[16] These are perhaps reminiscent on the Roman ban on generals crossing the Rubicon.

Chapter 5 by John Haldon is devoted to the political economy of empire. Haldon insightfully observes that empires are "both simple and complex" (p. 179). To be sure, hard power is hard power and military means remain paramount across all empires. The complexity is a corollary of the ever fluid exchange between the core area and the periphery, namely, the negotiation between local elites and rulers (p. 209). The Hittite empire was, for example, federated compared with the rigorously centralized Assyria (p. 180).

The greatest change to the makeup of empire occurred in the 15th Century, so one must acknowledge the fluidity of the concept. In this context, the conferring of citizenship on all free adult males in late Rome was an outlier in the ancient world. By contrast, the Portuguese empire arguably practiced slavery on a grander scale, and sought super profits through maritime trade rather than territory per se. It was a modern empire in that sense eager to monopolize key commodities, while pre-modern empire almost invariably relied on the agrarian sector for tax.[17]

Egypt in turn was a major source of grain for Byzantium (pp. 184–186, 193). Similarly, the Byzantine empire shifted the tax burden from cities to villages thus creating a new power structure (p. 213). However, it is very difficult to centrally collect tribute in the long run, hence, for example, the centrality of tax farming in the Mughal economy. It is also difficult to

up only 2.5% British GDP circa 1898. See also https://eh.net/encyclopedia/military-spending-patterns-in-history/.

[16] Hilde de Weerdt (2016), *op. cit.*, pp. 309–310.

[17] Thomas T. Allsen (2011), *op. cit.*, p. 363; Niv Horesh (2021), *Empire in World History: Commonality, Divergence and Contingency* (Palgrave), pp. 46–49, 83.

force peasants to pay cash rather than in kind (pp. 190–198). Sitta von Reden has observed in this context that in the pre-modern age:-[18]

> Taxation in kind continued to operate within the traditional institutions of collection and storage, but for cash taxes they gradually introduced tax farmers who came to be responsible for tax collection from the population itself. Tax-farmers played an important role in mediating between the economy in cash and in kind.

CULTURES OF POWER

In the 6th Chapter on pageantry, Cecily J. Hilsdale focuses on the use of Obelisks in the West and in the Byzantine and Ottoman empires, in particular, as a form of mystique borrowed from antiquity with which to legitimate empire. Here, a difference from Chinese empires suggests itself perhaps because the latter did not see such architectural cross-civilizational borrowing. Although both Chinese and Byzantine emperors were hailed as a sun, the latter had much more public visibility in for example hippodrome gatherings (p. 223).[19]

Borrowing from antiquity is all well but one might add that historical contradictions of empire abounded from day one. Rome was a foil to later empires but Polybius actually regarded its mission as the completion of Alexander the Great's venture. Rome had persecuted Christians and then enshrined Christianity—no less—as its *raison d'etat*.[20] In fact, Edward Gibbon went as far as asserting that Roman religious tolerance eventually brought the empire down.[21] The Byzantines broke away from Rome creating an alternative core. Yet they called themselves Romans, and the description would even cling to the empire that supplanted them in Asia

---

[18] Sitta von Reden (2015), "Global Economic History", in the *Cambridge World History* (Cambridge University Press), ed. by Craig Benjamin, pp. 29–54, f. 46.

[19] The Inca emperor was also likened to the sun; Chase-Dunn and Khutkyy on p. 166 of the volume under review also remind us that much like Chinese emperors, the Assyrian emperor was likened to a son of heaven (*mar banuti*).

[20] Krishnan Kumar (2019), *Visions of Empire: How Five Imperial Regimes Changed the World* (Princeton University Press), p. 12.

[21] Edward Gibbon (1857), *The History of the Decline and Fall of the Roman Empire* (Harper), *passim*.

Minor: the Ottomans. So much so that in distant China, the Ottoman empire was referred to as "Lumi" (Romi) well into the 19th Century.[22]

Polybius subscribed to dynastic cyclicality but argued that the Roman empire embodied good governance, and hence would avert decline. Herein lays the roots of Whig teleology: Polybius' views would be taken up by Machiavelli in the 16th Century, by English republicans in the 17th Century, by Montesquieu in the 18th Century and by the authors of the US constitution.[23] Polybius thus epitomizes the mystique of empire: the Romans like later empires, both pre-modern and modern, sought exalted forebears in the image of Alexander or the Trojans, so as to pre-empt decline. On his part, Rudi Giuliani famously declared US global leadership to be eternal, reflecting a sentiment once widespread sentiment among Americans.[24] All empires carry a sense of invincibility then. Yet even Kipling, the triumphalist poet of empire, warned that if complacent, the British empire could become a Nineveh or Tyre.[25] Triumphalism and anxiety go hand in hand.

Tacitus' *Germania* praised by contrast the roughness of Teutonic tribes. It later became a literary source and justification for German Protestants' revolt against Roman Catholicism in the 16th Century, and for German nationalism in the 19th Century.[26] More generally, Britain, France, Spain and—to a lesser extent Germany—all tapped into the mystique of the Roman empire in their own imperial ventures during the 19th Century, but at the same time, they later celebrated as emerging nation states perceived rebels against the very same Roman empire: Boudica, Vercingetorix, Viriathus and Hermann being the four best-known example.[27]

---

[22] Matthew Mosca (2013) *From Frontier Policy to Foreign Policy: The Question of India and the Transformation of Geopolitics in Qing China* (Stanford University Press).

[23] Michael Hardt and Antonio Negri (2001), *Empire* (Harvard University Press), p. 371; Daniel Woolf, *Concise History of History* (Cambridge University Press), p. 27.

[24] https://theconversation.com/the-end-of-americas-global-leadership-78736.

[25] Niall Ferguson (2004), *op. cit.*, p. 247.

[26] Daniel Woolf (2019), *op. cit.*, pp. 33, 55, 160.

[27] *Origiogentis* or the quest for exalted (putative) forebears with which to celebrate latter day polities is not confined to democracies. It begins with the Trojans who were appropriated by both the Roman and, later, the French in the Middle Ages. The quest was also evident in the Aryan preoccupation of Nazism.

This was not just a question of historical memory. From the outset, enthusiasts and detractors of empires vied for influence side by side. General Cincinnatus had famously waived dictatorship so as to pursue farming. At the heyday of empire, Augustus would by contrast see himself as a soldier, yet as enthusiasm for occupation declined—Diocletian would again invoke himself as a farmer.[28] A better known contrast perhaps is between Virgil, Propertius, and above all Horace, who celebrated Roman expansion, to Tacitus, Sallust and Calgacus who railed imperial excess.[29] In particular, Tacitus lampooned Nero's despotism decrying Rome's occupation of Britain as enslavement of the locals rather than their induction into civilization. Centuries later, Gore Vidal, echoing Tacitus, would decry the American empire as hijacked by militarism and tending to decadence.[30]

Against this background, Hilsdale valuably reminds us that obelisks or obelisk-like monuments can be found in many cities around the world including famously in Washington DC (pp. 230–238). Even the St Sophia Church in Kiev is partly inspired by obelisk shapes (p. 249), not to mention Delhi and Buenos Aires. To be sure, Ziggurats from Mesopotamia could not be transported as easily. And although Ottoman sultans' visibility was more limited than their Byzantine predecessors', with Topkapi palace as a kind of Forbidden City (p. 226), they kept the Byzantine Obelisk intact. All of that also reminds us that the Catholic Spaniards appropriated the Alhambra mosque, while the Muslim Ottomans appropriated Hagia Sophia with relative ease—again such cross-civilizational transference is hard to come by in the Chinese case.

In Chapter 7 on law and bureaucracy, Caroline Humfress reminds us in a similar vein that empire connotes unity in diversity (p. 267). That is to say, empire draws on varied sources of legitimation while professing singularity of rule and mind. The *millet* system of law in the Ottoman empire

---

[28] Christopher Kelly (2020), *The Roman Empire: A Very Short Introduction* (Oxford University Press), Kindle Location 967–971. See also Peter Frankopan (2015), *The Silk Roads: A New History of the World* (Bloomsbury), pp. 20–24. Virgil's *Anaeid* defended the imperial project. Horace was more triumphalist still seeking Roman dominion of the entire world including India and China.

[29] Stephen Howe (2002), *op. cit.*, p. 43.

[30] Niall Ferguson (2005), *Colossus: The Rise and Fall of the American Empire* (Penguin), p. 4.

granting religious minorities legal autonomy is a case in point, while the Mongol empire did not develop its own legal code at all (pp. 274–276).

The European joint stock trading companies had courts of law provided in their charters, and they went on to set up courts in their colonies (p. 279). Humfress rightly observes that these courts were popular with litigants much more than local courts because they were perceived as fairer. Often they would host trials between purely local protagonists. Even in South America Indians sued Indians under Spanish law for resource access (p. 281).

In Chapter 8 on cartography, Laura Hostetler clearly divides empires between pre-modern tributary polities and early modern ones. The former profess universal rule even when peripheral entities are acknowledged, and their depiction of the world is, therefore, fuzzy (p. 288). The early modern European powers were much more sensitive to the global balance of power and to specific demarcation lines. Their cartographic knowledge was standardized in part thanks to Jesuit observatories spread around the world that were only partly accepted by local rulers (p. 289). Matteo Rici, for example, introduced the concept of longitudes and latitudes to Ming officials, who had him produce a world map (pp. 296–303). In the Ottoman empire, Piri Reis similarly produced a map of the whole world including the Americas in the 16th Century but Ottoman map-making later fell behind.

The impetus behind European cartography improvement was medieval Italian city states requiring more accurate maps for navigation and trade. That knowledge then passed on to Portugal which began to bypass Ottoman trading routes by sailing toward West Africa. In the 15th Century, earlier classic geographical treatise like Ptolemy's were translated into Latin greatly enhancing European knowledge (p. 296).

Chapter 9 on religion by Amira K. Bennison traces the link between faith and empire. She argues that there is no empire without some form of religion but that generally Abrahamic religions played a greater role than say Buddhism in the formation of empires (pp. 318–319). Religion provides a "a circle of equity" or a moral code bounding rulers to look after society. Bennison also usefully reminds us that the role of religion was greater in pre-modern times where the divine was not doubted. Here one might add that historically *Realpolitik* trumped religion in bringing former foes together. Thus, the Ottoman empire was courted by many Christian powers to counter Russia. On the other hand, Ethiopian emperors almost always picked Christian allies.

Chapter 10 by Javed Majeed on literature discusses many imperial works, including of course the *Aneid* by the above-mentioned Virgil, which celebrated Roman power by juxtaposing it with Greece. Such works served as a template for so many subsequent empire builders. Literature played an important part in the education of imperial elites (p. 367). Majeed also usefully reminds us that although empires are usually repressive (p. 343), they are by nature multicultural and polyglot. The use of Latin was never imposed by Rome for example (p. 356).

Rome not Greece became the *locus classicus* of empire builders. But there were other means of support for empire builders too. The Spanish colonization of Latin America was likened to the Reconquista in literature, and British settlement in North America invited comparison with the earlier subjugation of Ireland. Yet, as Majeed argues, in dealing with Native Americans, Spaniards also resorted to the understanding of the earlier Roman encounter with Germanic barbarians (p. 353).

Disparities of Power

In Chapter 11, Burbank and Cooper, two of the most pioneering scholars in the field, broadly discuss hierarchies and elite co-option strategies. At first, they remind us that empires are large polities that aim at singular identity while incorporating diverse populations within their midst. By contrast, the world today is Westphalian, enshrining the equality of diverse nations. Yet the current phase is just a blip in human history where the former modality was usually the order of the day (p. 408).

To manage ethnic diversity, empires invent strategies under the rubric "the politics of difference" broadly aimed at reinforcing the superiority of the core area. These strategies can range from genocide of peripheral people to "treating difference [between the various peoples in the empire] as part of life" (p. 375). In between, the contributors seem to hint at the importance of divide-and-rule strategies (p. 387). One might recall, for example, that in the Spanish occupation of South America, the cultivation of ties with the internal enemies of the Aztecs mattered a lot in their defeat.[31]

The two extremes on that spectrum are arguably the Mongols, who entrenched racial differences, and the Romans, who at one point granted

---

[31] Andrew Marr (2012), *A History of the World* (BBC), p. 292.

citizenship to all male inhabitants of the empire regardless of ethnicity (pp. 379, 381). The Napoleonic empire also comes to mind as one granting equal rights to peripheral peoples, as well as perhaps successive Chinese empires' idea that being an insider could be culturally acquired rather than an inborn trait. On the other hand, the Mongols were more tolerant of other faiths relative to Christendom, and their legal approach was more hands-free. It remains the case that the early Russian empire learned a lot from them in managing multi-ethnic society (p. 384).[32]

The problem becomes vexed when considering that most empires required peripheral populations to serve in their armies. After all Punjabi troops—not Britons—were vital in suppressing the Sepoy Rebellion of 1857. Janissaries of course are another example of such injection of local power, and the famous turncoat Josephus Flavius reminds us that such dynamic persisted in antiquity too. Notably, the Carthaginian army was also mercenary based; the Ptolemaic dynasty relied in no small measure on Jews to defend and administer Egypt; Rome successfully recruited soldiers from among the Gauls and Greek; the Byzantines employed Spaniards and Vikings as mercenaries; and the army of Al-Andalus was similarly made of Berbers, not Arabs.[33]

In Chapter 12, Kim A. Wagner focuses on empire and the subaltern. He rightly observes that *Pax imperii* throughout history has been a myth because empire almost by definition invites resistance. Rebels against empires are celebrated today as proto nationalists but this was not always the case—some were seen as "mob" in the metropole at the time (pp. 417–418).

Wagner argues that the subaltern scholarly literature has overly emphasized armed resistance ignoring less overt acts of resistance (p. 423). He then focuses on the Sepoy Rebellion of 1857, remembered for its perceived atrocities by the British. Wagner sees "the dynamics of escalation" in anti-colonial struggle as momentous events that could be invoked to differentiate friend from foe. However, they were also everyday acts of non-violent resistance (p. 426). In the end, what mattered was that

---

[32] Mughal emperor Akbar was also famously tolerant of other faith with his concept of Din-I llahi.

[33] Andrew Marr (2012), *op. cit.*, p. 159–168, 221, 229; Simon Schama (2013), *Story of the* Jews (Bodley Head), p. 111, observes that contrary to modern perceptions in fact Jews were often mercenaries in the Ptolemaic-Seleucid world; See also Haldon p. 204 in the volume under review.

the East India Company could mobilize Indians of all classes to quell an Indian rebellion by using racial, caste and faith divisions.

The Maji Maji and Boxer Rebellions, on the other hand, show that (p. 428) in the high noon of imperialism colonizers convinced themselves that rebels could only react by falling into superstition. Indeed, the rebels then believed they were impervious to bullets. But Wagner suggests (p. 429) that the analyses of these rebellions should be placed in a wider social context. He finishes off by asserting that subalterns need not be essentialized through the lens of class struggle or proto-nationalism (p. 433).

Chapter 13 by Alf Hornborg is on empire and ecology. Hornborg argues (p. 437) that the ecological implications of imperialism are much more politically and morally charged than the famous Colombian Exchange might suggest. Yet Crosby's matrix (p. 438) naturalizes European expansion as purely a result of process of physical selection. These explanations leave out social science including economic history out of the equation. For when they are included, the Rise of the West supposedly narrows to an 18th-Century "accident" (p. 439).[34]

The chapter then sets the stage for the comparative analysis of metabolism of imperial subjects in different ages. It focuses on Han China, Rome, the Inca, the Aztec, Spain and Britain. The calculus here is difficult because in the 17th Century, for example, 60 percent of the immigrants to the New World were slaves, many of whom ended up in sugar plantations. Cheaper sugar as a result is thought by some to have facilitated the Industrial Revolution. Hornborg calls this "unequal exchange" (pp. 445–452). Notably, the US industrialized soon after Britain based on a similar mercantilist blueprint; yet the US was land rich and fuel scarce, while Britain was land poor and fuel (coal) rich. That is to say, different endowment led to the same outcome.

Chapter 14 by James Beattie and Eugene Anderson is on the environment too. Empires, they suggest, can be one of three: predominantly those based on fertile agricultural land, those based on maritime trade or shorter-lived nomadic steppe empires (p. 463).[35] Invariably, cold dry weather made empires retreat (p. 469), the Norse abandonment of

---

[34] Alfred W. Crosby Jr. (rep. 2003), *The Columbian Exchange: Biological and Cultural Consequences of 1492* (Praeger).

[35] On short-lived nomadic empires, see, e.g., Michael Gehler, Julian Degen and Robert Rollinger eds. (2020), *Short Term Empires in World History* (Springer).

Greenland being a case in point perhaps. Even the mighty Mongol empire succumbed to the Little Ice Age (pp. 469–70).

The contributors ably remind us that empires can change their surroundings through, for example, the construction of roads, irrigation and mining but can be equally unmade by flooding or disease, as Crosby's afore-mentioned classic study of the Columbian Exchange has shown (pp. 460, 467). The problem is that the academic literature on the interaction between empires and the environment before the Columbian Exchange remains scare (p. 461).

Part of the gap is closed here as the authors recount the disappearance of wildlife in Europe due to Roman hunting and circuses. They allege that the disappearance of wildlife in China and India was slower. At least in India that might have to do with Emperor Ashoka's *ahimsa* concept, which protected animals (pp. 466, 8).

Chapter 15 by Phiroze Vasunia deals with nostalgia for empire, which other contributors have touched on too. He starts off with the Ashoka Pillar in Allahabad which was appropriated by the Mughals despite the religious factor—Ashoka was Buddhist much early on, they were Muslim. And even though the Romans were the *locus classicus* of all future empire builders in the West, Vasunia reminds us like others that the Romans themselves looked to Alexander the Great (p. 499).

Vasunia then turns to the subjects of empire and their descendants, the founders of nation states on the ruins of empire. He recounts, for example, how prominently Prime Minister Manmohan Singh marked the 150th anniversary of the Sepoy Rebellion in 2007 casting it as a trauma which galvanized the modern Indian nation (p. 509).

The Volume is tied together by a final Chapter from prominent comparative sociologist John A. Hall. Rightly, Hall begins with the *leitmotif* of this book. He cites John Darwin to suggest empire was the most enduring form of polity in history (p. 523), thus one wonders how soon it might return on the world stage to replace the Westphalian model. The breakup of the USSR ushered in a final (?) triumphal wave of nation state creation (p. 524). Yet, equally, one must remember that empires are various in their makeup ranging from direct rule to the use of satrapies in antiquity, and from outright occupation to merely manipulating the terms of trade in the early modern era. This fluidity means the age of empire may not be over.

The problem of empire is that while it aims at universal rule in reality even the core area can often be composite, with Britain, the Danish empire and the Holy Roman Empire as obvious reminders (p. 525). Yet modern federal India, which is not imperial in nature, succeeded better in internalizing Tamil separatism (p. 537). What is more, imperial occupation does not always prove profitable, and the rate of return from colonial enterprise is usually normal at best (p. 526).

While Beattie and Anderson prize exogenous environmental factors in the rise and fall of empires, Hall seems to stress the moral factor, good governance, elite trust and taxation (p. 530). Here, famous Islamic thinker Ibn Khaldun immediately comes to mind again. He suggested empire builders were at first vital and viral but that triumphalism and riches then bring about decadence so that ruling dynasties become weaker over time, and lose the trust of the people.[36] Hall sensibly adds other explanations for the rise and fall of empires like military overextension, citing Paul Kennedy's famous study (p. 538).[37] He concludes by observing that—liberalism aside—the US is a unique empire based on the dominance of the dollar, which offsets global military costs.

In fine, the Volume under review exudes excellence in original research, ecumenical engagement and attention to detail. It will likely remain a beacon of high-end scholarship in the field of empire studies in the decades to come. The level of accuracy is compelling, all contributors speak with earned authority, and questionable points are few and far between.

---

[36] See, e.g., Peter Adams (2016), *Philosophy in the Islamic* World, p. 204.

[37] Paul Kennedy (2020 rep.), *The Rise and Fall of Great Powers* (Vintage).

CHAPTER 5

Establishing the Storylines

Abstract The field of empire studies has matured to the extent that this year it is buttressed by the publication of *The Oxford World History of Empire*, a set consisting of 2 volumes. This is a veritable milestone—a project bringing together the top authorities in academe for a discussion on divergence and commonality of empires across history. The dimensions here are truly global unlike the Eurocentric framework that blighted empire studies from 30 years ago. In that sense and in many other ways, this *History* is unsurpassed. Volume Two (*The History of Empires*) is an exhaustive assembly of case studies hammering discrete imperial storylines into one comparative storyline. It includes no less than 45 chapters on empires from the very beginnings of state formation in the Bronze Age up to the present. The chapters here are—in the words of the publisher—tied together by a set of synthesizing surveys that structure the world history of empire into eight chronological phases.

Keywords *The Oxford World History of Empire* · Volume Two · Peter Fibiger Bang, C. A. Bayly · Walter Scheidel

In recent years, historians have been shifting back much of their attention to empires after two centuries in which the nation state served as a touchstone of social-evolution research. This is driven by the recognition that we are still living in the shadow of our imperial pasts, and that today's global power brokers are not devoid of imperial ambition either. Nevertheless, much like the nation state, empire is not an immutable construct. As Philip Pomper argued, it is protean and ever relevant, particularly as nuclear proliferation may be changing the rules of the geopolitical game. Historically, many nation states turned into empires and changed back into nation states[1]—Athens and Carthage to be sure survived their imperial downfall for many years.

As mentioned, the field of empire studies has matured to the extent that this year it is buttressed by the publication of *The Oxford World History of Empire*, a set consisting of 2 volumes. This is a veritable milestone—a project bringing together the top authorities in academe for a discussion on divergence and commonality of empires across history. The dimensions here are truly global unlike the Eurocentric framework that blighted empire studies from 30 years ago. In that sense and in many other ways, this *History* is unsurpassed.

Volume One (*The Imperial Experience*) is of comparative-epistemological nature, and I have reviewed it in the preceding chapter. Volume Two (*The History of Empires*) is by contrast an exhaustive assembly of case studies hammering discrete imperial storylines into one comparative storyline. It includes no less than 45 chapters on empires from the very beginnings of state formation in the Bronze Age up to the present.

Peter Fibiger Bang, the first co-editor, contributed a Prolegomena, which also appears at the outset of Volume One, as well as the synthesizing surveys at the beginning of each phase. He perceptively observes (p. xxv): "Empire, it turns out, is truly protean and its lingering and deep history continues". Bang then (p. xxvii) suggests that following the late William McNeill historians must overcome their local biases so as to get at the bigger picture. But the case for comparative history (p. xxx) is not like the case for "connected" history, the latter dealing as it does with interstitial cross-cultural exchange rather than exchange between key agents.

Western theories of imperialism are mostly anchored in the circumstances of the early 20th Century with European domination at its height (they are covered in Volume One). However, the rise of China today

---

[1] Philip Pomper (2005), "The History and Theory of Empires", *History and Theory* 44.4: 1–27.

puts that early 20th-Century Western scholarship in perspective. Accordingly, in this Volume, the editors—Bang, the late Chris Bayly and Walter Scheidel—insist on the bigger picture but without imposing theoretical uniformity other than requiring all contributors to touch on military history and economic detail to some degree. This chapter will, therefore, have military and economic history at the forefront.

Part I—Bronze to Iron Age

In his opening survey, Bang presents Sargon of Akkad (f. 23rd Century BCE) as the first empire builder in history (p. 5). To be sure, Egypt had existed then too but was relatively self-contained with the exception of raids into Nubia and Palestine. Little is otherwise known of Sargon's empire: it was steeped in land cultivation where land was not plentiful so peasants could not run away easily from tax exactions (p. 7). Yet, notably, Sargon—not to be confused with the later Sargons of Assyrian stock—did not attack Egypt, a peer civilization/empire. Rather, it was the Hittites who checked Egyptian ambition in the Battle of Kadesh (BCE 1274). And because Assyria, centered on the famous Nineveh, and was the first empire to conquer Egypt temporarily (BCE 720)—one might suggest it should perhaps be counted as the first real empire in antiquity.

In a chapter on Egypt, Juan Carlos Moreno García stresses (p. 13) that even though pyramids had been built in Old-Kingdom Egypt (BCE 2686-2125) no real conquest occurred. Only later in the New Kingdom did conquest obtain, mainly in Nubia and the Syro-Levantine region. The driver for that conquest was the need for rare raw materials—tin was available only from Central Asia and wood for ships was to be found in Lebanon (p. 16). There was trade across the so-called Incense Road too. Egyptian exports included grain and gold, yet millet seeds found in Ukma suggest some contact even with China. Ironically, trade flourished in periods when the pharaonic state split into competing polities (p. 19), and that is perhaps reminiscent of the efflorescence of maritime trade in the Chinese Southern Song era.

In the Egyptian New Kingdom (BCE 1539–1075), which was more expansionist, mercenaries swelled army ranks and were involved in court politics (p. 35). Indeed, the centrality of mercenaries to empire building would reappear time and again in the following chapters. But the bulk of the Egyptian army was made of coscripts who at peacetime would be employed in agriculture, mining and building (p. 36). And in another formative *modus operandi* that would become global, the Pharos—who saw themselves as the center of the universe—kept princes from rival polities captive in their palace (p. 37).

Piotr Steinkeller in a chapter on Akkad and Ur reiterates (p. 43) that Sargon's was the first known case of empire building with his capital in the vicinity of modern Baghdad. The problem is few documents survive from the Sargonic era. Interestingly, though, the rise of Akkad occurred when in Babylonia city states were the norm—defying our European bias. That is to say, outside Europe, republic-like city states occurred frequently before the 1st Century CE, and Greece is by no means an exclusive case.

Sargon conquered those city states in Babylonia and then expanded into Anatalia and Iran with his predominantly conscript infantry (pp. 46–48). His rule was loose however—he left the internal administration of his new domains intact. One might add that that tendency too problematizes the notion that Sargon's was the first empire even if he called himself "absolute ruler".

Interestingly, Steinkeller suggests Akkadian ties with the Indus Valley via Tilmun (*sic*) were extensive. Indeed, profits from trade—not proselytization—were the main reasons behind Sargon's conquest (p. 52) even if—one might sardonically add—no joint-stock trading company existed at the time. And while Alexander the Great would become the template for empire builders, he himself admired Sargon in an early manifestation of *translatio imperii*.

Ur III was an empire which replaced Akkad on the world stage (p. 54). It is notable for devising the first codex of law in history, preceding Hammurabi's. It is notable also for the degree of centralization of land ownership under the monarch (p. 57), which seems to have exceeded Early China. The disposition of Ur III was defensive, avoiding large-scale conquest, imposing proportional taxation in the provinces and focusing on trade. Many foreigners served in its army. Though more centralized, Ur III was smaller in size than Sargon's domains thus it too hardly merits the epithet first empire.

Chapter 3 by Gojko Barjamovic on Assyria suggests trade continued to be a key driver of expansion: tin from central Asia was coveted, copper from Cyprus, silver from Anatalia, spices from Southeast Asia, gold from Egypt and aromatics from Arabia (p. 81). Notably, Assyria had a quasi-parliament at its inception, so again Greece is not alone. In its neo-Assyrian stage, critically, the empire conquered Egypt and Iran (p. 83), and it is those achievements as regards peer civilization/empires that arguably make it the true first empire in history. Yet, the Achaemenid empire would conquer Egypt long term.

The Assyrian empire co-opted ruling elites until its core became multi-ethnic (p. 84). Plots of crown land were distributed in return for military service, with the only indirect taxes imposed on imported goods—up to 25% (p. 84).

There were eunuchs at court too, and slaves were mostly domestic (p. 86). Compared with Akkad, the empire was still more decentralized. But some features were similar like the practice of holding captive princes in the palace (p. 93).

Chapter 4 on Persia by Matthew W. Waters stresses that Cambyses, the son of Cyrus the Great, conquered Egypt long term (p. 111), which arguably makes the Achaemenid empire the first true empire in history. Interestingly, Aramaic was the lingua franca of empire much like Greek was later used administratively by the Roman empire (p. 112). The early Persians were pastoralists hence they possessed group solidarity (*'assabiya*) much like the Arabs and Mongols later on. That is to say, they were thin on the ground at first but evolving into a mighty force (p. 116), a point reminiscent of Peter Turchin's famous study.[2]

Contrary to Egypt, Emperor Xerxes destroyed Athens but was unable to subdue the Greek world (p. 118). Nevertheless, Persians remained a force in Greek politics playing one city against another. In terms of conscription—land was given for service (*hatru*). Overall, the Achaemenids were considered tolerant because they kept local institutions intact and borrowed from all cultures.

Chapter 5 on Athens, Carthage and Early Rome by Walter Scheidel reminds us again (p. 137) that city states flourished not just in ancient Mesopotamia in the 1st millennium BCE but in all of the Mediterranean rim. However, Greece was the main cluster—not the Etruscans or Phoenicia. These Greek city states did hire mercenaries on occasion (p. 138) but mostly relied on its own population and on metics. The discovery of silver near Athens augmented its military buildup (p. 140) but its main defense mechanism was the famous Delian League. Unlike imperial structures, in the Greek city states core and periphery (homesteads outside city) were on par (pp. 139, 143).

---

[2] Peter Turchin (2009), "A Theory for Formation of Large Empires", *Journal of Global History* 4.2: 191–217.

By contrast, Carthage relied more on mercenaries (146). It started out as monarchy but later became more republican-like with a citizen army. There is no evidence the Carthaginian core was taxed at all (p. 149). Colonies were more rigidly controlled compared with other polities in antiquity (p. 151).

Early Rome like Athens and Carthage assumed prominence through alliance with other city states (p. 150). That did not prevent its early sack by the Gauls much like Athens was sacked by the Persians. Nevertheless, Roman citizenry expanded with subsequent occupations (p. 151).

Notably, mature Rome relied on food imports unlike Athens or Carthage (p. 155). And the periphery enjoyed tax breaks as a function of proximity to the core.

Part II—The Classical Age

In his survey of the classical age, Bang astutely quotes Tacitus (p. 162): "There can be no peace...without soldiers, no soldiers without pay and no pay without tribute". In that context, it is illuminating to note that the Roman army measuring several hundreds of thousands was surpassed in West Eurasia only in the 7th Century CE.

Chapter 6 by Christelle Fischer-Bovet on the Ptolemies and Seleucids stresses that both empires emanated from Alexander the Great, and both ruled around 200 years (p. 167). However, Seleucid territory was bigger and unlike some of its Mesopotamian predecessors left us abundant documentation mainly in the form of papyri (p. 170). In terms of world history encounters, the Seleucids ceded territory to Emperor Chandragupta in India in return for elephants (p. 171).

Astonishingly or not, military cost represented 78% of Ptolemaic revenue and 57% of Seleucid revenue in wartime, while the respective peacetime figure was 34% and 45%. Taxation was incidentally higher in Greece, and here perhaps Montesquieu comes to mind with his prediction that freer polities would exact more tax (p. 178). Tax farming (*telonai*) was rife in the Ptolemaic empire (p. 183).

Chapter 7 on the Mauryan empire (BCE 321-185) by Himanshu Prabha Ray stresses its unique place in Indian history with Emperor Ashoka in particular lionized by generations to come (p. 198).

Ashoka promoted Buddhism but probably did not enforce it. Yet there seems to be an inherent contradiction between the irenic devout Ashoka and the main political primer form that era, the Arthashastra, in that the latter is realist and cynical at times. It recommends, for example, the establishment of a secret police to root out opponents. Economically, the Arthashastra is reminiscent of Chinese legalist writings particularly when preaching state monopolies on mining (pp. 203–205).

Chapter 8 on the Qin and Han empires by Mark Edward Lewis stresses that universal conscription (p. 218) was the norm during China's preceding Warring State era. Like Ashoka, the First Emperor of Qin left inscriptions throughout the realm to assert his rule (p. 220). He famously standardized script, coinage, weights, and ordered the burning of heterodox books (p. 221). However, the First Emperor suffered imperial overstretch like Alexander the Great or Napoleon (p. 223). The subsequent longer lasting Western Han dynasty eventually abandoned universal peasant conscription (p. 224).

The Wu emperor of the Western Han dynasty also pursued hawkish policies, reviving state monopolies on salt and iron (p. 225). There was commutation of military service into tax, a professional army was established and military colonies set up (p. 229). In the Eastern Han dynasty, the peasant army disappeared completely and so did primogeniture. Local elites resurfaced, and rule was through elite cooption (p. 233).

Chapter 9 on Rome by Bang stresses that in the 8th Century BCE, it was one of many city states in the Mediterranean with a militaristic culture (p. 248). There had been early on like in Warring States China universal conscription (p. 249). In terms of imperial revenue, the Romans were less focused on trade and more on plunder, slaves and land tax (p. 252). By the Principate age, the army was reorganized as professional (p. 256). Like China, the land tax rate was moderate—around 5% of produce. Tax farming was minimized in the Principate era, and the Italian core was free altogether from tax (p. 267). Debasement was at times rampant (p. 271) as means to defray military outlay.

Chapter 10 by Matthew C. Canepa on the Parthian and Sassanian empires stresses that these two empires partly drew on Achaemenid precepts, but also forged new ideas (p. 290). They developed technology to stem the Roman advance on the one hand, on the one hand, and steppe nomads, on the other.

Byzantine-Sassanian relations stabilized under Husraw I (p. 298). He enacted a tax reform whereby much of the burden fell on the nobility, as well as means-based poll tax (p. 301). Earlier, tax on the Silk Road turned into a major source of Parthian income (p. 306). The cavalry was the backbone of the Parthian army, as well as Central Asian mercenaries

(p. 308). Mounted archers remained the backbone of the Sassanian army (p. 309), but religion was more strictly Zoroastrian (p. 311). Cuneiform script phased out during the Parthian empire too.

Chapter 11 by Craig Benjamin on the Kushan empire suggests the Kushans descended from the pastoral Tocharians (Yuezhi). Their best known ruler, Kanishka, was a Buddhist (pp. 325–328). But archaeological evidence is otherwise sparse, not least with the Taliban having ruined many museums and relics in Gandhara. The Yuezhi and Xiongnu both led semi-sedentary existence, however, from the 3rd Century BCE Xiongnu raids on the Tocharians made them undertake migration west to Kushana (p. 331). Han rulers in China sought in fact Yuezhi help in subduing the Xiongnu and sent to Kushana the emissaries Zhang Qian and later Ban Chao (pp. 333, 336).

The Kushan empire was finally destroyed by the Sassanians (p. 342). But the rise of monarchial and republican states in North India also impinged on the size of the Kushan empire: Naghas, Maghas and Yaudheyas (p. 343).

Part III—The Ecumenical Turn

In his survey here, Bang shows that despite Roman and Byzantine claims to universal rule they in fact compromised with the Parthian and Sassanian empires (p. 350) until the late 6th Century CE when a bubonic plague hit. This was followed by the rise of the Islamic empire from Gibraltar to Central Asia. Tang support for Buddhism makes therefore this age ecumenical with Christendom in the west, Buddhism in the east and Islam in the middle.

Chapter 12 by Andrew Marsham stresses that at its height the Islamic caliphate (p. 355) was twice the size of the Roman empire. The secret of early Islamic success was a distinctive monotheistic identity that united the leaders of the new empire. There were also widespread conversions among the conquered population.

Around 700 CE the Muslim advance was checked by Franks, Byzantines and Khazars (p. 357). But many among the conquered elites would join the Abbasid administration later on (p. 358). After the capital was moved from Umayyad Damascus, Baghdad became the biggest city in the world outside China with half a million inhabitants, and at the same time de-urbanization spreads in Europe (p. 361). African slaves and Turks were imported from the frontiers but they were mostly for domestic help rather than *latifundia* tillers. Abbasid total annual revenue was around half a billion dirham.

Chapter 13 by Mark Edward Lewis on the Tang stresses the fact that this dynasty lay the foundation for the Late Imperial Chinese empire, and featured many modern traits. The early Tang inherited the equal-field system from the Northern Wei state whereby land was redistributed to peasants. The military combined professional and conscripted soldiers. However, in the late Tang the military professionalized, and an exam system for public office was introduced. The center of gravity of the economy permanently shifted south (p. 381).

After the famous An Lushan Rebellion, tax was based for the first time in Chinese history on cultivable land alongside a revival of the salt monopoly from Han times. Yet Buddhist shrines were exempt from tax, and eunuchs were powerful at court (p. 384).

Chapter 14 on Srivijaya by John N. Miksic shows it to be a thalassocracy, or a constellation of ports in Sumatra (p. 401). In that sense, it was different to a land empire and more akin to Phoenicia, one might add. The study of Srivijaya, which means "glorious victory" in Sanskrit, is marred by the paucity of archaeological findings due to the wet climate (p. 404). The engine of the economy was the spice for metal trade it seems.

As early as 5th Century CE Srivijaya and other kingdoms in the Malay realm started sending tribute to China, yet China did not intervene in Malay politics (p. 406). To be sure, while China stood aside for the most part, the Indian kingdom of Chola did occupy Srivijaya for a time in the early 11th Century CE (p. 409). They even appointed a viceroy in Kedah (p. 420).

Chapter 15 by the late Michael D. Coe on the Khmer empire explains that the French colonial authorities in fact restored the long forgotten history of Angor Wat that had by then disappeared from Khmer collective memory (p. 430), and in that sense Srivijaya also comes to mind as it was unknown before the 20th Century. Today, ironically, Angkor Wat is on the Cambodian flag.

Indianization of the Khmer chiefdom seems to have begun in 1st Century CE (p. 435) but the India caste system only partly applied. The Khmer empire, which was initially made up of vassal kingdoms (p. 437), had no coinage—it exacted tax in kind and pursued barter. Hinduism gave way to Mahayana Buddhism later on but by 13th Century CE (p. 441)

Hinduism was back in vogue. The Khmer empire downfall was due to (p. 446) Thai migration southward.

Chapter 16 on the Byzantine empire by Anthony Kaldellis stresses that Latin served as the language of the administration right until the 6th Century CE (p. 450). After the Arab occupation in the 7th Century the empire became Roman ethnically, Greek speaking and Orthodox. Arab and Berber fleets conquered Sicily and Crete, but these were then retrieved in the 9th Century CE (p. 452). Following the Fourth Crusade (1202 CE), Byzantium was occupied by "Latins" who were expelled only in 1261 (p. 455). Tamerlane then defeated Sultan Bayezid (1402) extending a lease of life to the Byzantine empire by half a century (p. 456).

By the bestowal of citizenship, the fairly centralized Byzantine empire became meritocratic with few ethnic distinctions, and a number of emperors rose from below (pp. 457, 461). The Byzantines believed they were the only ones civilized, and that their empire in theory ruled the world (p. 459). Mercenaries, eunuchs and bishops were all involved in court politics. Taxes were relatively high based on poll and land taxes, and there was no tax farming. Overall, the empire's posture was defensive. Like in China there were eunuch generals, and the emperor who could be removed if losing trust—was also head of the Church (pp. 462–465).

Chapter 17 on the Carolingians by Rosamond McKitterick shows that future generations fought over the empire's halo: Charlemagne's grave for example was raided by Napoleon (p. 468). The legacy was further fought over between Catherine the Great and the Habsburgs. The Carolingians earlier on demanded tribute from the Bretons, and paganism was cited as the reason for their attack on the Avars (p. 473). Contrary to popular belief, Aachen in Germany was not an imperial capital, rather the empire was polycentric. The empire had standing army and annual assemblies (p. 476).

Part IV—The Mongol Moment

Bang in his opening survey stresses that the Mongol Moment is about nomads asserting their power over sedentary empires (p. 501). Genghis Khan (r. 1206–1227) was the most successful in consolidating nomad tribes into a mighty force that conquered and pillaged much of the Old World. By contrast, his successor Kublai Khan was tolerant and inclusive much like the Achaemenids. The Black Plague affected the manpower available to the nomads hence the division of the Mongol empire later on (p. 502).

Translated from Russian with few footnotes, Chapter 18 by Nikolay N. Kradin suggests (p. 507) that nomadic empires differed from agrarian ones in that the latter's metropolis did not have advanced economy and large population. Initially, nomadic empires lived by exacting tribute, trade tax and pillage in sedentary areas. What saved Europe from the Mongol onslaught was the death of Ogodei (p. 516).

In China, the Mongols relied on tax farming and then following a rebellion on proportional tax (p. 517). They encouraged religious diversity (p. 523). In West Asia, they bestowed *iqtaat* on their loyalists but in China they instituted a racial hierarchy in the administration with the famous *semu* foreigners on top and a token civil-service exam (p. 528).

Chapter 19 on the Ming empire by David M. Robinson is excellent. It goes against the grain of conventional wisdom which sees the Ming as an insular dynasty (p. 533). Founder Zhu Yuanzhang executed a suppression of society but his heir the Yongle emperor was more outward-going and spendthrift (p. 536). Zhu professed a return to ancient Shang and Zhou precepts but in reality retained many Mongol-era institutions like the hereditary military-duty households. Outwardly, however, he spoke of the eradication of "mutton stench" in relation to the Mongol warriors (pp. 537–538).

The Ming land tax rate was only 3% of the harvest and paid mostly in grain (p. 549). The army was between 1 and 2 million soldiers strong (p. 541), initially relying on household conscripts but after the 15th Century relying more and more on mercenaries and tributary forces (pp. 545–547). Robinson may be downplaying the 1578 Ming expenditure on defense at only 2.6 million taels.

Chapter 20 by the late Sunil Kumar stresses that the Mongols did not much intrude on the Delhi sultanate. Rather, the Delhi sultanate which was Turkic in essence checked Mongol raids (pp. 572, 579). Though highly monetized, the Delhi Sultanate was less grand than the Mughals (pp. 576, 581), theirs was a decentralized military government and many of the sultans were formerly slaves.

Chapter 21 by Jacob Tullberg on crosscurrents between Christendom and Islam stresses that both papal and Seljuk power on the eve of the crusades was federated (p. 598). The Byzantine on the eve of the first crusade merely wanted to protect Anatalia, but the crusaders wanted to reach Jerusalem. Saladin then deposed the Fatimids in Egypt but unlike the sultanate in Iberia recognized the Abbasid caliph (p. 607). Later caliphs nevertheless lost the power that the Rashidun caliphs had had. Beginning in the 12th Century CE kingship became identified with jurisdiction and less with faith (p. 615).

Chapter 22 on the Venetian empire by Luciano Pezzolo shows it emphasized its independence from both the Holy Roman Empire and the Byzantine empire (p. 621). After the fall of Constantinople, Venice—like Muscovy—fancied itself as a second Rome. From the 14th Century CE, the Venetian leader—the doge—was elected by 200 patricians sitting in the senate (p. 623).

In competition with Genoa, Venice acquired colonies from the Istrian peninsula to the Black Sea (p. 624). Venetian ships used artillery—the navy was manned solely by locals including convicts (p. 631) but the land army included many mercenaries. Venice benefitted from colonies by, e.g., distributing to them salt for higher price (p. 626). Crucially, unlike most land empires, Venice state revenue came mainly from indirect taxes on trade and consumption (p. 634). Military outlay took up about half of the budget (p. 638).

In Chapter 23 on the Mali and Songhay empire, Bruce S. Hall suggests that the Muslim literature produced in Timbuktu rivaled that produced in the Middle East (p. 648). This goes against the Hegelian stereotype of Africa as "Land of Childhood". Songhay (1464–1591 CE), the most cohesive of African empires, was able to defeat a Moroccan expedition. But the Songhay administration was otherwise decentralized except for the control of trade in, e.g., slaves, gold, Chinese silk and porcelain (pp. 651–652, 660).

Part V—Another World

In his opening survey, Bang explains that the pre-Columbian empires were "another world" because they lacked wheeled transport, iron tools and horses. Chapter 24 by Michael E. Smith and Maëlle Sergheraert on the Aztecs shows (p. 671) that Tenochtitlan was the largest city in America when the Conquistadors arrived. The Aztec empire regularly extracted tax and gifts based on landholding over several million people but Cortés toppled it with little effort (pp. 672, 679, 685).

Aztec society formed as city states from 1100 CE. All men received military training in their youth so they could be called up anytime (p. 676). Swords were made of obsidian, and money consisted of textiles, bird feathers, gold jewellery and cacao beans (pp. 679, 681). Kings were elected by a council (p. 683). The form of administration over city states other than Tenochtitlan was indirect (p. 687).

Chapter 25 on the Inca empire by R. Alan Covey suggests it formed between 1400 and 1530 CE, not long before the arrival of the Conquistadors (p. 692). It straddled several climates and had no writing system but instead used the famous *qipu*. The Incas were preceded by the Moche, Wari, Tiwanaku and Chimu states. However, by 1400 CE the Inca achieved dominance through marriage, diplomacy and military conquest (p. 698). Yet they often allowed local lords who recognized their dominance to remain in place (pp. 704, 706).

Like the Aztec, The Incas practiced human sacrifice (p. 700). Like elsewhere in the ancient world, the Inka king was deemed the son of the sun, with the main sun ritual located in Cuzco. The Incas were also known for their storehouses (*qollqa*) designed to supply soldiers with maize staple (pp. 702, 709).

Part VI—The Great Confluence

Bang states here that the Iberian powers drew a lot on the Venetian colonial model, including the use of gunpowder (p. 725). In Chapter 26 on the Ottoman empire Dariusz Kołodziejczyk shows that by the 16th-Century Istanbul was one of the largest cities in the world (p. 737). Generally, the Ottomans dealt well with the crusaders but were crushed by Tamerlane (p. 731). The great setback of the Ottoman empire was the naval defeat at Lepanto in 1571 (p. 729). Until Aurangzeb's accession to the Mughal throne, the Ottomans claimed to represent all Sunni Muslims.

The Ottomans relied on *sipahi* cavalry who enjoyed usufruct but no jurisdiction over plots of land (*timar*). So this was different than European-style or Russian-style feudalism. In addition, primogeniture was embraced in succession contrary to nomad blood tanistry (p. 733).

The annual revenue of the Ottoman empire in the 16th Century was larger than France—between 7 and 10 million gold ducats (p. 737). Tax receipts were both in kind and in cash. Eventually, the *timar* system was abandoned, and the army professionalized. In the late Ottoman era, there was great reliance on tax farming (p. 744).

Chapter 27 by Rajeev Kinra on the Mughals stresses that at its height their empire was as big as Europe with twice the population (p. 751). This pluralistic dynasty died out in 1857 following the great Sepoy Mutiny (p. 739). The dynasty saw itself as heir to both Tamerlane and Genghis Khan (p. 753). The most prominent ruler was Akbar the Great who initiated the *sulhi kull* precept bringing together Muslims and Hindus (p. 755). Land was resurveyed under the Mughals and turned into the *zabt* tax farming system replacing *iqtaat* (pp. 767–768).

Chapter 28 by Josep M. Delgado and Josep M. Fradera on the Habsburg empire stresses the composite nature of the empire (p. 789). Charles V abdicated in 1555–6 in favor of his brother and son (p. 792). Defeat of the Spanish Armada by the British put great pressure on the empire for reform. The empire failed in its bid to occupy Algiers (pp. 794, 807). In South America, fifth of the colonial profits flowed to state coffers under the *encomendero*; alcohol monopoly was instituted, as well as the venal sale off state posts (p. 799).

Chapter 29 by Pamela Kyle Crossley on Qing China stresses the thrifty nature of the empire rulers (p. 810) as explaining its longevity. The empire was secured by multi-ethnic 500,000 bannermen—half were Chinese. This is reminiscent one might add of the recruitment of local sepoys in India by the British (p. 814).

The Qing bureaucracy drew heavily on the previous dynasty, the Ming (p. 817). There were 3 government monopolies: in silk, in ginseng and in salt (p. 822). But the size of the Song state relative to population was double that of the Qing (p. 825). Taxes were low in part to avert rebellions—in the 18th Century the rate was no higher than 8%, and the bureaucracy employed only 200,000 officials (p. 827).

Chapter 30 by Francisco Bethencourt on the Portuguese empire suggests it was the longest-running of all modern empires—established in 1415 at the conquest of Ceuta and dismantled no sooner than 1999 in Macau (p. 832). More than 1.6 million people left Portugal for the colonies between 1415 and 1822 (p. 836). The model for later Portuguese colonies was Madeira which became the biggest sugar plantation in Europe in the 15th Century (p. 837). Of course after 1570 Brazil became the main source for sugar to the metropole. Crucially, from 1500 to 1800 most of the empire revenue came from trade (p. 840).

Portuguese cartographers changed European notions of time and space—e.g., Reinel and Homem (p. 850). Most of the slaves in the New World were transported by Portugal (p. 851). However, Portugal was expelled from Ethiopia in 1634 and from Japan in 1638 (p. 852). Portuguese joint-stock trading companies would be established only later in the 18th Century—unlike the British and Dutch model, trade was state monopoly (p. 856).

Chapter 31 by Leonard Blussé on the Dutch empire indicates that by the mid-17th Century the Netherlands was a nation of only a million inhabitants but that its merchant navy was larger than all other European nations combined (p. 862). Many Dutch had in fact worked for the Portuguese before sailing around the Cape of Good Hope. The Dutch empire was devoid (p. 864) of missionary zeal unlike the Iberian colonial enterprises.

When the Spaniards sacked Antwerp in 1585 (p. 865) Amsterdam became the leading financial hub in Europe. Other than its massive trade with Asia and the Americas, the Dutch empire also had extensive trade with the Baltic region (p. 858). In fact, the Dutch East India Company (VOC) turnover represented only about 15% of overall Dutch foreign trade.

The VOC went bankrupt due to a costly war with the British between 1780 and 1784 as well as due to innate corruption (p. 875). Because the Caribbean was more accessible to interlopers, the Dutch West India Company (WIC) was less monopolistic. But it went bankrupt earlier in 1674 due to losses in Brazil (p. 879). Unlike the British East India Company, the VOC rarely relied on Dutch naval support in times of war (p. 880). There were fewer Dutch migrants to the pertinent colonies than other nations because despite congestion the standard of living in the Dutch metropole was high.

Chapter 32 by Nicholas Canny on the First British empire suggests (p. 884) that the origin of the empire lay in pirating off Atlantic waters against Spain, while assailing at the same time Spanish attitudes to Native Americans. The boilerplate of the British colonial project was initially Ulster—Scots were more drawn there than to the Americas (p. 887). Raleigh and Cromwell's hawkishness explains the tilt toward further flung colonies (p.890).

Part VII—The Global Turn

In his opening survey, Bang reminds us that European colonialism eventually subdued the old agrarian empires (p. 911). Europeans had fought for "free trade" around the world but that included opium and slavery (pp. 914, 916). At any rate, the triumph was not long lasting as by 1820s the winds of self-determination had started blowing in South America.

The watershed was Napoleon's rise, which upset the balance of power in Europe. Out of the wreckage of empire—both agrarian and modern—emerged nation states (p. 912). The latter still define the contemporary world.

Chapter 33 on the British empire by the late CA Bayly is for the most part lecture notes given in Barcelona a few years ago. Contrary to the conventional wisdom casting modern empires as short lived, Bayly reminds us that the British empire lasted 400 years (p. 921). He warns us against overstating the non-settler component of the empire: in 1890, for example, Australia consumed as much British textile as the whole of India (p. 925). For Bayly, the secret of success of the British empire was "light touch", i.e., buying off local leaders rather than occasional genocidal policies (p. 930).

It's important to recall Scots and Irish, both Catholic and Protestant, supplied migrants to the empire much more than the English proportionately. For example, in 1830 some 60% of white settlers in India were Irish Catholics, who often spoke Gaelic and had their own ecumenical hierarchy. Similarly, the Anglican Church was disestablished in Australia as the main church in view of the large Celtic population (p. 931).

Chapter 34 by David Todd argues that there is ambivalence in France today (p. 941) as regards the imperial enterprise because it is seen as deviating from the principles of nation statehood. In the past, the *mission civilatrise* was the logic of the colonial empire buttressing European superiority (p. 942). In theory, the goal of empire was assimilating within the French state the colonies as *départements*. Whereas there was much racial fluidity in Canada, in Algeria where French settler numbers were proportionately higher there was much racial discrimination (p. 944).

French migrant numbers were relatively low except for Algeria, and the French empire never achieved the kind of colonial halo that the British or Dutch enjoyed (p. 946). The American Revolution impacted the outbreak of the French Revolution, and the latter did not see the definitive end of slavery in French colonies (p. 951). However, a successful slave revolt did break out in Haiti.

Despite the image of Napoleon's army as one of mass conscription, up to 60% of the soldiers in Napoleon's army were foreign (p. 952). Tax extraction under Napoleon circa 1800 was just 10% of national income, notwithstanding the abolition of tax farming (pp. 953–4).

Contrary to Republican values, the Third Republic in fact extended French formal empire in Africa and Indochina (p. 957). There is a dispute over just how much the colonies contributed to the Third Republic with some estimates putting the figure at merely 5–10% of foreign trade (p. 959).

Chapter 35 on the Russian empire by Dominic Lieven notes that following the demise of the Byzantine empire in 1453, Muscovy became the only independent Orthodox power, and its rulers started calling themselves Tsars (caesars) (p. 964). However, Ivan the Terrible's overreach into the Baltic region ended in disaster. It was Peter the Great who secured the Baltics for Russia at Sweden's expense (p. 695). His army was based on a mix of conscription and irregular Cossacks (p. 967). There were later 650,000 Russian soldiers and 230,000 militia fighting against Napoleon (p. 968, 971) with most soldiers being peasants conscripted for 25 years.

Chapter 36 on the late Spanish empire by Josep M. Fradera stresses that (p. 991) precious-metal mining was at the heart of the Spanish colonial effort in the Americas. African slave trafficking was contracted out (p. 922). In the late 18th Century, an alcohol and tobacco monopoly augmented government revenue (p. 995) but induced rebellions (p. 997). The monopoly on tobacco was abolished in the 1850s (p. 1004). Interestingly, the American population of the empire was represented at the Cádiz *Cortes* (p. 1000) following Napoleon's occupation of Spain.

Chapter 37 by Amy Greenberg on the US in the 19th Century reminds us that it had initially been an Atlantic polity (p. 1011) with European powers controlling the rest of the continent. Building and disavowing empire at the same time, the US expanded territorially very quickly in the 19th Century on the back of the Manifest Destiny ideology (p. 1013).

Initially, the US military was very small and distrusted by the young republic but it grew during the Civil War (p. 1014). Between 1846–8, the US fought a successful war against Mexico gaining much new territory (p. 1035). After the Civil War, the US army was reduced again from 1 million to just 29,000 combat troops (p. 1030). In 1890 a revival of the Manifest Destiny occurred after the ideology went into decline during Civil War: war with Spain in 1890 gained the US still more territory (p. 1031).

Chapter 38 on Native American nomads' kinetic empires by Pekka Hämäläinen argues that the last great nomadic empire was not the Mongols' but that with extended over the vast American grassland: the Comanches and Lakotas, based as they were on imported horses (p. 1035). That is to say that in the middle of the 18th Century the Comanche reinvented themselves as equestrian nomads (p. 1036), hunting bison. This quasi empire did not seem to have regular tax collection, but it raided rivals for loot (p. 1038).

Based in New Mexico, the Comanche reached their apex in the early 19th Century as US traders would come to their domain in search for horses for muskets (p. 1041). They were decimated by an outbreak of smallpox between 1788–1816 (p. 1044), and experienced steep decline after 1840 due to drought, disease and US pressure to settle them in reserves (pp. 1048–1049).

The Lakota Sioux also experienced ascendancy in the early 19th Century (p. 1050) in the Northern Great Plains. In the 18th Century, they had tried to build ties with French traders in beaver pelts for guns. They then started mounting horseback in the course of the early 19th Century (p. 1051). Like for the Comanche, the bison was staple for the Lakota, but for hides not for food. In 1876 the Lakota defeated the US army in the famous Battle of Little Bighorn (p. 1053). This galvanized the US government to subdue them once and for all.

Chapter 39 by Michael A. Reynolds and Rana Mitter argues that both the Ottoman empire and Qing China were ultimately crushed by foreign debt (p. 1055). However, there was arguably less resistance to fiscal reform in the Ottoman empire as it was closer geographically to Europe (p. 1063). In both empires to be sure there were traditionalist elements opposing Western encroachment—the *bektashis* in Turkey and the boxers in China. The institutions foisted by the West were similar in both empires—most notably customs administration, capitulations and "extrality" (p. 1318).

Chapter 40 on the Sokoto Caliphate by Murray Last states that this empire in modern Nigeria was independent until the early 1900s, then turned into a British princely state (p. 1083). Its origins are in a jihad declared by Shaikh Usman in 1804–1808 against local pagan custom (p. 1086). The Caliphate relied on cavalry perhaps in contrast to the image of the region (p. 1084).

The empire did not mint coinage and instead used Maria Theresa thalers, north African dinars and cowrie (p. 1087). Many slaves were included in the army, and their armory incidentally was made of cotton like that of Inka soldiers (pp. 1092–1094). The caliphate was divided into semi-independent emirates (p. 1103). The Sokoto Caliphate was also plagued by a sense of impermanence, and for this reason and others is not considered by Last a full-fledged empire (pp. 1105–1106).

Part VIII—The 20th Century

Bang surveys here the collapse of empires and rise of superpowers in the 20th Century. He notes how despite Wilsonian ideals circulating, the world has witnessed 3 catastrophic imperial contests: two world wars and a cold war (p. 1113). Upon the collapse of the Soviet Union in 1991, the US stood alone as a unipolar superpower.

Paradoxically, the end of World War I saw the British and French empires expand territorially with mandates in the Mideast (p. 1115). That said, the Suez Crisis of 1957 was the turning point in which the US forced imperial Britain and France to retreat (p. 1119).

Bang believes that because the US was more market-led than the USSR it was less reliant on territory. Yet the rise of China at present signals the end of US unipolarity (p. 1112). In our world, sovereignty and equality among nation states are sacrosanct but the distribution of power to be sure is anything but equal.

Chapter 41 by Hedinger and Brescius is on the German and Japanese empires. Both empires in the authors' view were megalomaniac and short live (p. 1123). As early as 1874 Japan sent a punitive expedition against Taiwan, while fast integrating Hokkaido and the Ryukyus within its territory. As early as 1876, Japan signed an unequal treaty with Korea (p. 1128). Japanese colonies were more settler-oriented and contiguous than Germany's (p. 1132).

German colonial efforts in turn were driven by a search for markets and raw materials (p. 1130). Yet in 1913 the colonies contributed only 2.55% of German GDP. German trading firms failed in East Africa and were replaced by direct state intervention (p. 1131). Hitler forsook the dream of having overseas colonies altogether (p. 1141) and this led to a convergence of interest with Japan. Strangely, for all his racism, Hitler decided to ally with Muslim peoples in Eurasia (p. 1154).

Chapter 42 on decolonization and neocolonialism by Stuart Ward suggests empire is a concept that is notoriously difficult to pin down because of its mutability over time (p. 1161). Ward, too, points to the Suez canal crisis as the watermark when empire began to unravel (p. 1164, 1172). In turn, the origin of decolonization was emancipation in Latin America in the 1820s. This begot a long process till the establishment of the League of Nations whereby empire was partly replaced by nation states. Part of the pressure for decolonization stemmed from the fact that colonials had no mobility rights like citizens of the metropole (p. 1169).

Jean-Paul Sartre coined the term neocolonialism in 1956, and the notion empire was creeping back did shoot up after the assassination of Lumumba in 1961 (pp. 1176–7). Neocolonialism then became entwined with dependence theory in the 1970s (p. 1180). Today, Chinese firms in Africa are often labeled neocolonial because they are seen as deindustrializing local economies.

Chapter 43 on the USSR by Geoffrey Hosking stresses that it was unusual empire in that it dispatched its message to all of humanity but followed "socialism in one country" (p. 1187). The USSR also subsidized colonies (satellite states) at the expense of the metropole although here it was no different than the US (p. 1203). Yet a Soviet consumption tax further subsidized heavy industry and impoverished consumers (p. 1192). Following the dekulakization drive of 1929, famine struck in 1931, and in addition by 1938, 700,000 died as a result of political persecution (p. 1193). Stalin reversed the verdict on the Tsars and praised their contribution to nation building (p. 1197). When Gorbachev took power, whopping 40% of the government budget went to defense (p. 1210).

In Chapter 44 on America's global imperium, Andrew Preston reminds us that the US is not a normal nation: in 2011 its defense budget surpassed the next 13 countries combined with 300,000 soldiers stationed overseas (p. 1217). However, while Russia today embraces its imperial legacy, the US is still in denial about its imperium. The uniqueness of American power is that it sways the foreign policy of other nations (p. 1221), but usually avoids meddling in their internal affairs. This is the essence of the international liberal world order that was ushered in by America in 1945 through multilateral for a like the UN, Bretton Woods, GATT and IMF and the World Bank.

The US not only occupied the Philippines and Hawaii far from its shores, but would also intervene in countless conflicts in Latin America (not to mention Iran). Even Wilson deployed troops to Mexico twice (p. 1231). Yet the 1930s were later a time of isolationism, and Roosevelt would famously declare the US did not covet any foreign territory. If USSR spent 40% of the GDP on defense, the figure was closer to 10% in America's case (p. 1237).

Chapter 45 is an Epilogue by Frederick Cooper. Like Bang, he reflects on the fact that even though the equivalence of nation states is enshrined in the liberal world order (p. 1249), the distribution of resources is far from equal. For these reasons, for example, some African leaders do not settle for nation statehood but actually strive for "metropolitan" citizenship (p. 1250). Ironically, Germany and Japan failed as colonial empires but prosper as nation states (p. 1259). The breakup of empire, Cooper adds, does not mean that states now neatly align with nation—indeed many peoples remain stateless (p. 1265). Finally, Copper seems to hint that globalization is here to stay at the expense of state sovereignty (p. 1274).

Overall Appraisal

There is much to admire in this Volume, not least in terms of global and spatial coverage. Bang assures us that he as first editor endeavored to include all empires worthy of the name, yet inevitably some borderline cases fall by the wayside. Other stories are included although the case for empire is not clear-cut, e.g., the Comanche confederacy or the Sokoto Caliphate.

Of the 45 chapters, none was devoted, for example, to the Maya civilization, presumably because this was more a case of competing urban hubs than a single hegemon. But many empires that fit the bill more tightly are absent—the Gupta empire, the Götürk khaganate, the Tibetan empire, the Vikings, the Chola empire, the Burmese empire, the Timurid empire, the Safavid dynasty or the Gaza empire to name but few.

Because its focus on economic history, this Volume ought to be read alongside another edited volume of much comparative value, *Fiscal Regimes and the Political Economy of Premodern States*, edited by Andrew Monson and Walter Scheidel (Cambridge University Press, 2015). *Fiscal Regimes* suggested, for example, that per capita taxes in England in 1776 were 25.6 times than in China. Prior to that, pre-modern states had relatively low tax revenue and spent little other than on defense. Often tax was in the form of corvée labor or in kind rather than monetized.

But taxation in the pre-modern world could rise: in Principate Rome there was a shift away from tax farming toward cadastral-based levies. There was also a spike in taxes in Song China, Ptolemaic Egypt and the Byzantine empire.[3]

---

[3] Philip T. Hoffman (2017), Review of *Fiscal Regimes*, *Journal of Economic Literature* 55.4: 1556–1569.

Like Qing China, the Mughal administration was miniscule compared with the population (p. 773). And like Song China, the Mughal government provided loans to peasants to upgrade seed and equipment (*taqawi*) (p. 774). Tax breaks were similarly given in times of drought, and grain was dispensed. Beyond India and China, one is reminded that famine relief was also to be found in the West although perhaps less widely. The Chinese case is well known, what with the "ever normal granaries". But in Rome too the *Cura Annonae* supplied subsidized wheat imported from Egypt to commoners.

In terms of taxation, early modern Venice was an outlier in that indirect levies on trade and consumption provided for the bulk of government budget (p. 634). Venice instituted a salt monopoly but that was not a rarity in the ancient and early modern world. Neither was the ratio of defense a rarity: military outlay took out about half of the budget (pp. 635, 638). A standing army was established in the 15th Century, but the government bureaucracy was proportionately small (pp. 641, 643).

It seems to follow from the Volume that several social practices died hard in the early modern period: first, the enfeoffment of land in return for military service; second, the holding of captive princes as insurance policy against rebellion by domestic or foreign rivals. Likewise, eunuchs and mercenaries were important power brokers right until the 19th Century. Marriage as a form of cementing royal alliances also disappeared only in the 20th Century.

Our modern bias suggests modern representative politics emerged in Renaissance Italy but were rooted earlier on in the Greek city states. Yet a wider reading of world history shows democracy's roots are much more extensive than Greece, and include, for example, Babylonian city states as well as the common practice of tanistry, at least in nomadic empires. Even the Aztec emperor was elected by a council.

Bouda Etemad's classic *Possessing the World* (Berghahn, 2007) shows—based on tentative data—that in the long run modern empires cost little, and were economically insignificant to the metropole. We still have no data with which to check this in antiquity. But this accords with the broader literature which shows warfare in modern Europe was many times more painful to the metropole than suppressing revolts in the colonies. Of course, foreigners to begin with played a much bigger role in overseas forces.

Notably, the economic takeoff of France in the 1970s occurred after it had shed many of its key colonies. Yet Robert Allen decisively showed in *Global Economic History* (Oxford University Press, 2011) that England would not have grown rich without deindustrializing India. Intuitively, I lean toward Allen: it may be that the figures representing colonial goods in the ledgers were stated down.

THE JEWISH DIMENSION

In a powerful recent article in *Haaretz*, prominent Israeli historian and public intellectual Yuval Noah Harari declared that "Judaism is not a major player in the history of humankind".[4] He, therefore, called for modesty in appraising the Jewish contribution to the world before the 20th Century.

Certainly, reading the Volume under review would tend to reinforce Harari's claim. One does find the Jewish Rebellion that led to the destruction of the Second Temple in the Index but this is it. Jews are mentioned here and there elsewhere but never as lead players.

What is more, things we tend to conceive of as distinctly Jewish appear in different guise. Isaiah and Ezra's commendation of Cyrus, for example, is in fact reminiscent of Xenophon.

Assimilation anxiety is another example. Early on, the Assyrian empire co-opted ruling elites until its core became multi-ethnic (p. 84). Plots of crown land were distributed in return for military service, with the only indirect taxes imposed on imported goods—up to 25% (p. 84). But over the centuries there had also been detractors of multi-ethnicity as a form of "core" dilution.

Arguably, Jewish self-perception as regards assimilation pressures is one of tenacity. The Volume might remind us though that Jews had been very Hellenized around the Common Era. Jewish identity prevailed despite occasional Byzantine attempts at forced conversion. And that beyond Kaifeng, there are other little-known episodes of assimilation like that of the Lançados Jews in Africa (p. 838). This alongside better-known conversions into Judaism like that of the Khazars.

Besides tragic eviction, what comes across from the Volume is the Jewish knack of being at the right place at the right time. In the early 13th Century, there had already been Jewish presence in the key port city of Barus, Sumatra, for example (p. 414). That is to say that Jews

---

[4] https://www.haaretz.com/jewish/.premium.MAGAZINE-judaism-not-A-major-historical-hero-1.5417341.

both arrive early and would later follow European imperialists around the globe.

In this context, where Harari may be going too far has to do with the Inquisition. Jews contributed much to Iberian prosperity. When they were expelled from Lisbon, many moved to Amsterdam helping making the latter the new finance hub of Europe. Amsterdam was the crucible of modern liberal Europe long before the 20th Century.

Where Harari may be right concerns the Holy Land. Anyone raised in Israel's state school system would tend to associate it pretty exclusively with a numinous re-settlement by Jews in later times. But world history books like the Volume under review insist on the appellation "Palestine" in view of the long hiatus between the destruction of the Second Temple and the first wave of Zionist migration. In between, from world history perspective, "Palestine" does not matter religiously as much as, for example, in it being the site of the Battle of Ayn Jalut (1260). Readers who have reached thus far but are at a loss at the sound of this Battle may be products of the Israeli state school system. For the Battle is key event in world history and should be taught at school early on so that the end result is more inclusive.

CHAPTER 6

Academics, Politicians, the Media and the Making of Modern China's Worldview

Abstract This chapter will focus on two books that deal with academe and media narratives in the main. The chapter will begin with Xin Fan's important and fascinating *World History and National Identity in China: The Twentieth Century* (Cambridge University Press, 2021), and move on to Christopher A. Ford's equally impressive *China Looks at the West: Identity, Global Ambitions, and the Future of Sino-American Relations* (University of Kentucky Press, 2015). Both books are enriched by primary material but chart a partly well-trodden path.

Keywords Xin Fan · Christopher A. Ford · National Identity

How is one's sense of foreign countries created? Part of one's national identity, it is presumably shaped by what our family tells us irrespective of whether they themselves have been overseas or not; it is then molded by our own overseas experiences if we ever go overseas. Then, especially if we do not travel frequently, our worldview is shaded by what we see and read in the media, and on a deeper level—what we are taught at school and university. To be sure, family sentiments and overseas travel are notoriously difficult dimensions to survey in a country like the PRC, and the pertinent literature here is thin.

This chapter instead will focus on two books that deal with academe and media narratives in the main. The chapter will begin with Xin Fan's important and fascinating *World History and National Identity in China: The Twentieth Century* (Cambridge University Press, 2021), and move on to Christopher A. Ford's equally impressive *China Looks at the West: Identity, Global Ambitions, and the Future of Sino-American Relations* (University of Kentucky Press, 2015). Both books are enriched by primary material but chart a partly well-trodden path. In Fan's case, Dominic Sachsenmaier, Dorothea Martin and Xu Luo's work immediately come to mind; in Ford's case—David Shambaugh, Zhang Biwu and Wang Jianwei spring forth among others.[1]

Fan's book is divided into four chapters: one loosely on the late Qing, another on the Republican era, the third and fourth are on the 1950s–1960s, and the fifth on post-Mao China. Thus, the contemporary and near-contemporary angles are allocated less space except for the Conclusions. Ford's book is also chronological for the most part but it has more coverage of the Xi era even if it was published earlier. Part I is broadly on Sino-American perceptions in the Late Qing era. Part II is on the Republican and early PRC eras. Part III is on the Deng era. Part IV is on the immediate post-Deng era. Parts V and VI are loosely on the Hu Jintao era. And Part VII is on the Xi era. Here, the Cultural Revolution and its impact on Sino-American perceptions are accorded less space.

* * *

Reaching across different periods in modern China, Fan's book is not only good intellectual history but also part of the "global turn" in disciplinary terms. As mentioned, the topic itself is not new but the book-length treatment, broad temporal scope and cited archival materials make it special and a joy to read. In a word, the author sets out to explain the field

---

[1] Dominic Sachsenmaier (2011), *Global Perspectives on Global History: Theories and Approaches in a Connected World* (Cornell University Press); Dorothea Martin (1990), *The Making of a Sino-Marxist World View: Perceptions and Interpretations of World History in the People's Republic of China* (ME Sharpe); and Xu Luo (2010), "The Rise of World History Studies in Twentieth-Century China", *History Compass* 8.8: pp. 780–789; David Shambaugh (1993), *Beautiful Imperialist: China Perceives America, 1972–1990* (Princeton University Press); Zhang Biwu (2012), *Chinese Perceptions of the U.S.: An Exploration of China's Foreign Policy Motivations* (Lexington Books); Wang Jianwei (2000), *Limited Adversaries: Post-Cold War Sino-American Mutual Images* (Oxford University Press).

of world history in China by way of contributing to a more holistic world history. So, the history of world history is front and center, but navel-gazing about world historians is never an issue.

To explain the field dynamics, Fan's approach is to focus on historians rather than students of history, and there is here far more about academic debates than on classroom discussions or textbooks—the latter dimension is covered by Martin. For example, Martin brilliantly shows that in the early 1970s, due to Maoist prescripts, the role of peasants in events such as the English Glorious Revolution was inflated.[2] The intellectuals mentioned are otherwise mostly familiar names to specialists but there are also lesser known figures.

At heart among these intellectuals is a select group of Chinese world historians from various backgrounds and how they tried to counter Eurocentrism as well as ethno-centrism (pp. 8–9). This is not usual: in all countries, there are worldly critics of chauvinistic textbooks and national narratives as well as Eurocentrism.

The first part of the book zooms in on those who believed then in the "common nature of humanity". They insisted that China should be treated organically as part of the rest of the world in an environment where there was separation between "foreign" and "Chinese" history. World history as a discipline became part of the curriculum only in the Republican period.

In the 1950s, the discipline was under heavy Soviet influence, coming of age (p. 18) as it did then. Soviet influence meant that all histories were subjected to the Marxist 5 stages of human development beginning with the primitive and slavery, and training was conducted in Russian instead of English (p. 18). Further, in the 1950s, world history became a compulsory topic, and textbooks were translated from Russian (pp. 22–23).

Fan asserts that despite the heavy Soviet influence the older guard of lecturers who had been trained in the US and Europe could sometimes prevail over younger Marxist teachers. And that academic professionalism was cherished (p. 29). Although the early 50s were known to be relatively open, more research needs to be done in that direction.

---

[2] Dorothea A.L. Martin (1990), *The Making of a Sino-Marxist World View: Perceptions and Interpretations of World History in the People's Republic of China* (M.E. Sharpe), pp. 45–50.

Fan sometimes labels intellectuals quite confusingly, and jumps from one period to another and back—famous historian Lei Haizong (d. 1962) is a case in point (p. 30). It is not clear if Lei was a liberal, fascist, conservative or leftist. Then, Fan turns to Zhou Weihan (d. 1910) who was the first to truly compare patterns in Chinese and world histories (pp. 31, 57–65).

A traditional physician by training, Zhou, who scarcely read foreign languages, wrote the popular *Outline of Western History*. This was apparently the incipience of Chinese global identity despite the research flaws. Importantly, he used Chinese periodization rather than the Gregorian calendar, and described human nature in neo-Confucian terms. In that sense, he did not succumb to Eurocentrism at a time China was weak. All humans without difference of race, according to Zhou, shared basic features: sexual desire, caring for youth, respecting elders, selfishness, contentiousness, seeking repute, attraction to beauty, competitiveness, fear of disasters and pursuit of comfort.

Zhou disagreed with conservatives who claimed the West got rich by stealing ancient Chinese wisdom (pp. 66–67). Audaciously he argued that Egypt had been more advanced than ancient Shang China, but, on the other hand, suggested Confucianism was a superior moral system able to unify the world (p. 69). In his analysis, China stagnated because Europe was better at exchanging ideas and embracing science.

It is hard to determine precisely how influential Zhou's book was, and more evidence might have been adduced here. One needs to recall that (p. 45) other important work had circulated in China to do with foreign knowledge beginning with the Jesuits and later protestant missionaries, and then material translated from Japanese. The treaty ports were particularly receptive to such translations.

Fan's description of Liang Qichao is quite positive because Liang among other things had written on ancient Greece from a Confucian perspective, or in other words was less taken by Rankean nation state models, or Eurocentrism. He argued Western power could not be deciphered without understanding Greece (p. 51). This is very different to Ford's description of Liang as totalitarian, as will be discussed later.

Fan's coverage is fairly extensive when it comes to the PRC except for the Cultural Revolution. In the post-Mao era, there was generally less Marxist and more nationalist exegesis yet on the upside more nationalism meant less Soviet-era Eurocentrism (p. 33).

Chapter 2 zooms in on the Republican era at greater depth. Fan points to the fact that the leading world historians at the time—Chen Hongzhe, He Bingsong and Lei Haizong—had all been trained in the West unlike Zhou Weihan. They were particularly influenced by American empiricism (pp. 91–92). But state presence at schools and universities in the early Republican era was low compared with the Communist era. "Foreign history" was introduced into the school curriculum later in 1929 but research on the subject was scant (pp. 98–99).

Lei Haizong was definitely a rising star. He was research oriented and increasingly radicalized by the Japanese invasion of China in 1931, moving from liberalism to an anti-Eurocentric position. Because of that, he was also a critic of H. G. Well's famous *Outline of History*. Lei's was a complex approach: notwithstanding his anti-Eurocentrism, he knew China in turn was not inexorably great in all periods, and he felt uneasy about national-grounded histories (pp. 110–115).

Fan does discuss Lei's call for a re-militarization of the Chinese spirit to meet the challenges of the age (p. 118) but does not discuss Lei's ideas about the Chinese polity suffering from *wubing de wenhua* or excessive irenicism. This is a shame because this idea has returned to Chinese discourse in the 1990s (see, e.g., the discussion of Wang Xiaodong in Ford's book below). Further, Lei's *Zhanguo Clique* generally praised legalism over Confucianism and was tainted with fascism (pp. 123–126).

Eventually, Lei chose to stay in the PRC even though Chiang Kai-shek personally invited him to Taiwan (p. 172). But he rejected the famous Marxist 5-stage formula in historical evolution (p. 226); Lei was tangled up in the Hundred Flower campaign for bemoaning the lack of textbooks at his university, and for excessive reliance on USSR. In the end, Lei was declared a class enemy and dismissed from his professorship.

Chapter 3 turns our attention to the early Mao era at greater length. It revolves around Li Zhichun who is considered the founding father of ancient world history in the PRC, and went on as "red professor" to shape the field in many ways. Despite relative freedom for figures such as Li, Fan reminds us that Yan'an rectification methods were applied in Chinese academe at the time to bring lecturers to heel, e.g., through collective criticism sessions. Thus, academic autonomy was under threat (p. 154). In addition, the Kafedra model was imported from the USSR engendering more collective research and rigid professionalization along time periods (p. 158).

But after the Sino-Soviet split there was an about face, and in 1961, world history was taken out of the curriculum in junior high schools. Then, during the Cultural Revolution, amateurism was lionized, and themes of class struggle pervaded world history writing. Chinese and foreign histories thus became more segregated from one another (p. 164, 171). On the other hand, a World History Institute was established in 1964.

Chapter 4 is largely a repetition of themes discussed in the previous three chapters, along with a survey of Chinese Marxism. The universality of historical materialism was stressed in the early 1950s while the Western-trained old guard of intellectuals stressed Chinese exceptionalism (p. 218). There is here coverage of the debate on the Asiatic Mode of Production (AMP), an issue covered by many previous studies. Notably, after 1957, the AMP came to be doubted in USSR too (p. 238).

Chapter 5 deals with the post-Mao era. On the one hand, world history returned to school curriculum in 1978 but few universities offered the subject at first. In 1979, Li Zhichun's important outline of the ancient world was published, revisiting the debate around the Asiatic Mode of Production (p. 286). Some scholars went further by arguing that city states and democracy were not unique to the Greco-Roman world but could be found in Sumer and to a lesser extent China. Then, following the Tiananmen Massacre, Chinese approaches to Chinese history became less comparative in nature (pp. 254–255, 275, 283, 359).

The conclusions cast a sidelight on the field of world history in China today, where Confucian exceptionalism is back in vogue. The side-effect is that Chinese history is again being segregated from world history in some quarters, and national and period professionalization reign (pp. 314, 317). Be that as it may, Fan's argument is that a history of world history in China is a contribution to world history as a whole. Despite Globalization there is a danger of losing sight of the bigger picture with growing specialization (323). Today there is, however, much money pouring into world history research.

Fan claims the latest school textbooks integrate Chinese and Western history into single narrative (p. 334), but my research suggests this is not the case at junior high level. There is great political sensitivity around this. For example, as Ford recounts (p. 27), the journal *Bingdian* was shut down in 2005 because of an article which suggested middle school history textbooks are over-nationalistic, playing up China's humiliations at Westerners' hands.

Overall, the book is well written but repetitive at times. There is a sense that periodization could have been better organized—the May Fourth era and the later Mao era seem to have received scant attention. The Xi era with its iteration of the "China dream" is also understated, at a time when China is striving to lead Globalization. Finally, the historicity of the arguments could be enhanced: for example, there is no source to buttress the claim that upon conquest of China the Qing cracked down on neo-Confucianism (p. 43).

* * *

While Fan deals with academe in the first instance, Ford deals more with the party-state propaganda narrative and the popular level in terms of perceptions of the outside world. China guards the narrative tightly because it believes the USSR disintegrated precisely because it allowed too much self-doubt to creep in. Yet the title of Ford's book is misleading, as he seldom treats the European dimensions and only segues to deal with Japan briefly. So "Looking at the US" would have been a better description of the content. Ford also employs colorful tropes like the Great Telos of Return, and the Sutras of Modernity that tend to obfuscate intellectual debates more than they can reveal. Liang Qichao's designation as "Confucio-Leninist" (p. 6) is particularly problematic, as his defense of autocracy was far from unequivocal. Liang is usually known as a reformer, and he was also an admirer of George Washington.

Like many other scholars, Ford observes that China has a love-hate relationship with the US, that is China aspires to become as strong as the US but opposes it on the world stage (p.2). Under Xi Jinping, it is actually positioning itself to replace the US. This confidence is because the GFC (p. 7) made the West look unstable thus unfit to teach China, causing some psychological dislocation.

The first part is broadly on the state media. Ford recounts that Party institutions in charge of propaganda and thought work are enormous and tightly guarded of all the bureaucratic systems (*xitong*) in China (p. 14). The reform era is thought to have diversified the media but when it comes to political content (as opposed to entertainment) Ford is unimpressed with the level of openness in the PRC. He concedes though that changes ensuing from commercialization have widened the sector. In 1978, there were only 186 newspapers and 930 magazines published. By 1986, however, these figures had reached 1574 and 5248 (p. 19).

Censorship is tight. Journalists are given detailed instruction on what theme they can cover, including verboten words and concepts, and on the other hand what issues to promote. These are regularly updated. There is a gradient of topics along these lines, as well as blacklists—one is reminded of Liu Xiaobo here (p. 24).

The Arab Spring and the Colour Revolutions were a particularly touchy theme in China as they indicate the cause of democracy has not weakened in the world, as Party propaganda claims. In those circumstances, terms like Civil Society were banned in the news (p. 26).

Of late, there has been an attempt to include public opinion surveys and readers' feedback in the Chinese media by way of demonstrating openness. The historical petition system has also been reinstated, along with village elections. Ford argues, however, that Chinese surveys are unreliable. Because of repression, polling in China—he argues—is generally flawed—particularly when conducted by foreign scholars (pp. 56–57).

Ford rightly stresses that Chinese perceptions of the US are Janus faced. On the upside, many Chinese show "amazement and envy" at American scientific and technological achievements (p. 97). This interest goes back to the May Fourth movement which was anti-Sinocentric, championing the cause of "Mr. Science and Mr. Democracy".

Earlier in 1903, leading reformer Liang Qichao visited the US and found it perplexing (p. 104–105). Ford claims this shook his belief in democracy, as he witnessed much disorderliness. Liang concluded freedom could lead to social disintegration. Ford laments Liang perceptions about America but considering the "robber barons" and segregation of that age for example, he might not have been completely deluded. Even Westernized liberals like Lin Yu-tang claimed in 1936 that democracy was "…a little ridiculous" (p. 111).

Moving onto the early Mao era, we have to note that the Korean War greatly deteriorated Chinese perceptions of America due to incessant propaganda. The US was depicted as hellish but at times also as a paper tiger. This vein of propaganda was dialed down only after Kissinger's visit to Beijing in 1971 (p. 118).

Through much of the early Deng era (1978–1997), there was a concerted effort to improve relations with the US after PRC isolation in the Cultural Revolution. Deng spoke of America favorably, even donning a cowboy hat in a visit to Houston in 1979 (p. 145). China's posture at the time was that of an avid and even somewhat submissive pupil, and the policy was one of "keeping a low profile".

Such sentiments culminated in the late 1980s. The famous Chinese TV documentary River Elegy (*Heshang*) is a case in point because it argued that "Chinese culture was not adequate to the challenge of pursuing national glory in the modern world" (p. 165). However, the driver of this critique was an urge to seek national glory through reform so as to counter the "aggressive" West. These sentiments were paralleled with a new propaganda line championing the re-Confucianization of society at the expense of Marxist hermeneutics (p. 171).

The Tiananmen Massacre of 1989 was a veritable watershed, as it led to more pronounced nationalism in the media and to more "patriotic" education at school level. On the one hand, there was talk of "national humiliation" (*guochi*) caused by Western and Japanese imperialism, and on the other hand, reports on the West suggested the freedom of speech there was fake (p. 192). This was supposed to induce indignation that would lead to greater support for the Party in its bid to restore China's glory. Crucially, this trend ran counter to the Maoist-era narrative which was all about China "standing up" and proving victorious.

This victim narrative had a profound impact on Chinese society and could be seen playing out in many anti-Western and anti-Japanese demonstrations and boycotts since 1989. But ironically, on the sidelines, there were also new veins of pro-Western thought like those to do with appreciation for the role religion and spirituality play in American life (p. 251). In response, the Chinese government encouraged the spread of prescribed religion in society.

Chinese self-confidence recovered beginning in the 1990s. When Japan fell into its Lost Decade in 1991, there was much triumphalism in China (p. 233). This led also to generally steeper anti-Japanese sentiments. China remained largely unscathed by the Asian Financial Crisis of 1997. Then, when the 2008 Global Financial Crisis struck, there was again much jubilation in China, leading many to conclude America was a spent force (p. 332). Nationalism strengthened on the back of the 2008 Olympic Games successfully held at Beijing, where China almost topped the medal tally.

Today, democratic reforms are off the agenda. Under Xi, the Party has shifted toward unapologetic authoritarianism. Firebrands such as Wang Xiaodong are allowed to harp on Chinese victimization by the West, and to declare the US and world capitalism cannot be trusted (p. 311). Like Lei Haizong, Wang calls for the reinvigoration of China's martial spirit, "…articulating a neo-Darwinian view of the world that saw international conflict as ennobling, and imagined China, after a purifying struggle, finally coming out on top of the global pyramid".

It seems the Party's new Confucian (and nationalist) narrative has not captivated big crowds outside China. There is one exception though: Daniel Bell, a Canadian-born professor at Shandong University, and self-avowed Confucian. He loosely believes that Western pluralist democracy of the one-person-one-vote variety is unequal to the challenges of modern political life. In his view, democratic elections tend to produce instability and are unable to provide effective decision-making because voters tend to consider short-term interests at the expense of broader concerns.

Greater allowance for the Confucian propaganda narrative also meant the present was couched in terms of time-honored Chinese traditions. Thus, for example, even socialism was said to have roots in Chinese antiquity where the private sector co-existed with a strong state sector (p. 355). In international relations too, there has been an effort to develop Chinese distinct theories, drawing in particular on China's Warring State era which is thought to be most similar to today's Westphalian system of competing nation states (p. 371).

Conspiracy theories regarding the US are aplenty in China. For example, when President Obama called in 2009 for the abolition of nuclear weapons—something that had been a staple of Chinese foreign propaganda for years 26—Chinese described it as a devious trick. Obama's disarmament posture was supposedly a plot to force countries like China into submission, because of deficiency in conventional forces (p. 374). Moreover, under Xi Jinping, China has taken a harder line on Taiwan in late 2014, with Xi publicly repudiating the so-called 1992 Consensus on Taiwan by describing the PRC—Taiwan relationship as one of "one country, two systems" (p. 408).

Over the years, China has argued it could change the world for the better as an alternative leader to the USSR or America because unlike them it was unhegemonic. In other words, Chinese analysts argue China can democratize the uneven current liberal international system, presided over by the US, not least because of China's developing-country credentials. The Chinese claim the US may be democratic domestically but that it acts unilaterally on the world stage (p. 429). However, beyond clichés on Confucian harmony reigning, the specifics of China's alternative world order—what institutions will govern and how, etc.—remain vague (pp. 435, 439).

According to Ford, the problem with Chinese prescripts is that they talk much about harmony and non-interference but in reality, cannot tolerate criticism even beyond China's borders. Increasingly, in recent years, China has sought to intervene and punish elements overseas that lend support to the Dalai Lama or Taiwan, or indeed to Uighur separatists (p. 457). In turn, the Party has invested a lot over the past decade in soft power overseas—through the establishment of scores of Confucius Institutes, or by setting up global television network in English (p. 455). Indeed, pressure of Chinese sanctions has led to self-censorship in Hollywood and elsewhere.

In the last part of the book, Ford offers some policy implications for US government officials' ears. Unlike China "huggers", Ford believes the US should penalize China for adversarial behavior, including presumably negative propaganda for domestic consumption. He calls for greater involvement of the Department of Defence in formulating the administration's China policy (p. 481). In essence, this sounds like containment including greater military deterrence. At times, it sounds as if Ford believes a conflict is inevitable, and calls for preparation sooner rather than later (p. 482). Drawing on John Garver, what he rightly finds ominous here is that Chinese military writing on Taiwan never seem to include the option of defeat.

Nevertheless, beyond the American fanfare about democracy, Ford does concede that from a realist point of view, China and the US could clash even if the former democratized (p. 500). This is a brave suggestion which increases the book's value. Other than pinyin mistakes, Ford has given us a flowing account of the Chinese worldview. It is a joy to read, and an instructive companion to Fan's book from a more contemporary angle.

CHAPTER 7

Conclusions

Abstract Only nuanced assessment of empires can lead to a profound understanding of the Rankean historical construct of the nation state. The nation state is not disappearing even if some imperial traits are coming back to the front stage. So-called reemergent empires like China are arguably multi-ethnic nation states. On the other end, the Trump era persuaded many around the world that globalization was over—even NATO was at risk. Yet President Biden did much to reinstate America's global alliances.

Keywords Empire · Nation state · China

The idea behind this short book was to provide an accessible snapshot of the bustling field of world history, with particular emphasis on empire studies. We began with a review of Olstein's theoretical exploration, and agreed with his basic intuition that good world history requires out-of-the-box thinking. The nation state is the Rankean bugbear of world history in that regard, as its framework was superimposed on researchers through much of the 20th Century. Yet we also admonished against airbrushing nation states from historical accounts as they are still vital to our lives.

Suffice it to note the sentiments they stir every 4 years in the Olympic Games. Our lives have been unrecognizably transformed by Globalization, but the particularities of the nation state still overrides global citizenship. This world belongs to nation states. However, there are some 8,000 nations and only 193 members in the UN.

Olstein showed how the particularities of one nation state—in this case Perón's Argentina—can be rewritten globally through various lenses. He takes the reader on a journey to Brazil, Egypt and Indonesia among various other nation states in search of instructive comparisons and connectivity. In doing so, he paints a more coherent picture of post-war populism. He also traces the enduring impact that Britain had on the Argentinian economy.

Finally, one of the strengths of Olstein's book is that it is wary of teleology, whereby democracy is supposedly the end point of history. Here, he mentions in passing the convolution of governance in Rome and, more importantly, the fact that disenfranchised minorities in democratic societies often look up fondly to non-democratic countries. Thus, for example, African-American infatuation with Japan transpired, particularly during the inter-war era.

On a similar theme, Kumar observes that there is today popular nostalgia for empire. 59% of Britons say they are proud of the achievements of the British empire for example. In Turkey, China and Russia too the imperial past is being rehabilitated. It is no longer cast as feudal or autocratic. Yet, the enthusiasm for empire in the Russian, Chinese and Turkish case is very much top-down. There is no discernable appetite for the return of British rule in India, or other parts of the colonized world for that matter. There is similarly no great appetite for the return of empire in Hungary and Austria. And the BLM movement has demonstrated that even in "core" countries the legacy of empire is vexed.

For Kumar empires in antiquity lacked a universalist ideology, they were merely preoccupied with occupation and domination. Yet, much like Chinese emperors, the Assyrian emperor was likened to a son of heaven (*mar banuti*), a universalist epithet. More to the point, Kumar draws clear distinction between pre-modern empires and modern ones. As Adam Smith observed, the discovery of the Americas was a watershed in history. Notably, pre-modern empires were land based, modern empires had blue navies to straddle the ocean.

Is the US a different kind of empire, e.g., an "Empire of Liberty" in Jefferson's parlance? On that score, as we have seen, Immerwahr argued that US technological breakthroughs during the post-war era made formal empire unattractive to the US in view of the rising tide of national liberation movements worldwide. First, greater blue water mobility through, for example, the Panama Canal and aircraft carriers made holding on to large swathe of territory with ground forces less compelling. Faster planes have made the deployment of ground forces easier too.

Kumar's final point is that nation states cannot simply be the be-all end-all of history because they spread anarchy and violence. He seems to hint that we are witnessing the withering away of the nation state, but as previously argued, this is far from obvious. Besides, many nation states are nowadays ethnically composite not unlike empires "from within".

Hall's chapter in Volume One of The *Oxford World History of Empire* was particularly instructive in that sense because it showed the longevity of empires arose from moral factors, good governance, elite trust and rationale taxation. On the moral factor, Ibn Khaldun immediately comes to mind. He suggested empire builders were at first vital and virile but that triumphalism and riches then bring about decadence so that ruling dynasties become weaker over time, and lose the trust of the people. Hall sensibly added other explanations for the rise and fall of empires like military overextension, citing Paul Kennedy's famous study. He concludes by observing that—liberalism aside—the US is a unique empire based on dominance of the dollar, which offsets global military costs.

If Volume One is the capstone of The *Oxford World History of Empire*, Volume Two provides the nuts and bolts of the analyses, not least in terms of economic history. There is much to admire in this Volume, not least in terms of global and spatial coverage. Bang et al. clearly strove to include all empires worthy of the name, yet inevitably some borderline cases were omitted.

It's worth recapitulating per capita taxes in England in 1776 were 25.6 times than in China. Prior to that, pre-modern states had relatively low tax revenue and spent little other than on defense. Often tax was in the form of corvée labor or in kind rather than monetized. But taxation in the pre-modern world could rise: in Principate Rome, there was a shift away from tax farming toward cadastral-based levies. There was also a spike in taxes in Song China, Ptolemaic Egypt and the Byzantine empire.

Early modern Venice was an outlier in that indirect levies on trade and consumption provided for the bulk of government budget. Venice instituted a salt monopoly but that was not a rarity in the ancient and early modern world. Neither was the ratio of defense a rarity: military outlay took out about half of the budget. A standing army was established in the 15th Century, but the government bureaucracy was proportionately small.

Several social practices died hard in the early modern period: first, the enfeoffment of land in return for military service; second, the holding of captive princes as insurance policy against rebellion by domestic or foreign rivals. Likewise, eunuchs and mercenaries were important power brokers right until the 19th Century. Marriage as a form of cementing royal alliances also disappeared only in the 20th Century.

Many people think modern representative politics emerged in Renaissance Italy but were rooted earlier on in the Greek city states. Yet a wider reading of world history shows democracy's roots are much more extensive than Greece, and include for example Babylonian city states as well as the common practice of tanistry, at least in nomadic empires.

There is a linkage between this Volume and Xin Fan's book in that both show conservative Chinese in the 19th Century believed Western science had been derived from ancient Chinese wisdom.

Xin Fan shows in his turn how world historians like Lei Haizong interpreted Chinese history as lacking in martial spirit. Like many of his generation, Lei chose to stay in the PRC even though he could comfortably relocate to Taiwan. This is a reminder that the CCP was more popular in early 1950s in the Chinese-speaking world. Nevertheless, in the end, Lei was declared a class enemy and dismissed from his professorship.

On the one hand, world history returned to school curriculum in China in 1978 but few universities offered the subject at first. In 1979, Li Zhichun's important outline of the ancient world was published. Some scholars went further by arguing that city states and democracy were not unique to the Greco-Roman world but could be found in Sumer and to a lesser extent China. Then, following the Tiananmen Massacre, Chinese approaches to Chinese history became less comparative in nature.

Like Lei Haizong, many nationalists in China today call for the reinvigoration of China's martial spirit. Thus, Ford does concede that from a realist point of view, China and the US could clash even if the former democratized. This point is a harsh reminder as to why scholars need to continue studying world history. It is only through civilizational comparison that we can discern the shared origins of democracy as well as its limitations over the years. Whether Lei was right in calling China an irenicist society is another matter that will require separate inquiry.

Ford may think clash between China and US is inevitable but the picture is more complex. It is true that the "victim narrative" of the 1990s had a profound impact on Chinese society, and could be seen playing out in many anti-Western and anti-Japanese demonstrations and boycotts since 1989. But ironically, on the sidelines, there were also new veins of pro-Western thought like those to do with appreciation for the role religion and spirituality play in American life. In response, the Chinese government encouraged the spread of prescribed religion in society. So, clash apart, there are also signs of convergence in an increasingly Globalized age.

* * *

As I have argued earlier, the interplay between the process of globalization and the staying power of the nation state is slippery. And the challenges posed by climate change require a new level of global coordination even if voter mood in many parts of the world is turning nationalistic.

Only nuanced assessment of empires can lead to a profound understanding of the Rankean historical construct of the nation state. The nation state is not disappearing even if some imperial traits are coming back to the front stage. So-called reemergent empires like China are arguably multi-ethnic nation states. On the other end, the Trump era persuaded many around the world that globalization was over—even NATO was at risk. Yet President Biden did much to reinstate America's global alliances.

Clearly, globalization is an imperial construct. Thus, American tilt at isolationism during the Trump era was a tilt at the nation state, and a move away from Eurocentrism. On the other hand, today, with China risen, the return or so-called return of empire is associated with the notion that Eurocentrism may be bowing out from the historical front stage. The Global South is deeply studied nowadays, but English remains firmly the language of instruction.

How will this inform US-China relations in the future? It's hard to tell but conceptually one needs to determine whether the competition between the two giants is Globalization-conducive, imperial or national in its character. If it is imperial in its reach, then it must spread globalization too. Yet, both the US and China's economies have retreated nationally in recent years, not to mention COVID-19 closures and student visa cutbacks. Secondly, China has very few friends and only one formal ally. In that sense, its imperial reach is mostly or purely economical. It is too early to suggest China's rise betokens the return of empires. Yet, given its rich imperial past, it won't be a surprise either if it turns out this way.

Printed in the United States
by Baker & Taylor Publisher Services